ANOTHER TIME

Books by Eli Mandel

Trio (with Phyllis Webb and Gael Turnbull)   1954
Fuseli Poems   1960
Poetry 62   Ed. with Jean Guy Pilon   1962
Black and Secret Man   1964
Criticism: The Silent Speaking Words   1966
An Idiot Joy   1967
Irving Layton   1969
Five Modern Canadian Poets   Ed.   1971
Contexts of Canadian Criticism   Ed.   1971
Poets of Contemporary Canada   Ed.   1972
Eight More Canadian Poets   Ed. with Ann Mandel   1972
English Poets of the Twentieth Century   Ed. with Des Maxwell   1972
Crusoe   1973
Stony Plain   1973
Out of Place   1977
Another Time   1977

This book is Volume III in the series
THREE SOLITUDES: Contemporary Literary Criticism in Canada
A series on the literatures of separation — ISSN 0701—8339

I.	*Articulating West*	Wm. H. New
II.	*Caliban Without Prospero*	Max Dorsinville
III.	*Another Time*	Eli Mandel

porcépic

ANOTHER
TIME

eli
mandel

Copyright © 1977 by Eli Mandel
Published in June 1977 by Press Porcepic Ltd., 70 Main Street, Erin, with
the assistance of the Canada Council and the Ontario Arts Council.

Cover design by Hester Bell
Printed and bound in Canada by the Hunter Rose Company

1   2   3   4   5   80   79   78   77

Distribution:

CANADA	U.S.A.	U.K. & EUROPE
Burns & MacEachern Ltd.	Press Porcepic Ltd.	Books Canada Ltd.
62 Railside Road	70 Main Street	1 Bedford Road
Don Mills, Ontario	Erin, Ontario	London N2
M3A 1A6	N0B 1T0	England

Canadian Cataloguing in Publication Data

Mandel, Eli, 1922-
    Another Time

(Three Solitudes: Contemporary Literary Criticism in Canada); 3;
ISSN 0701-8339.

ISBN 0-88878-076-1 bd.   ISBN 0-88878-077-X pa.

1. Canadian literature (English) — History and criticism — Addresses,
essays, lectures.*
2. Literature — History and criticism — Addresses, essays, lectures.
I. Title   II. Series.

PS8077.M35   C810'.9   C77-001274-4
PR9184.6.M35

Contents

"A painting is a space in which we see another space; a poem is a time which permits another time, at once fluid and motionless, to be seen. Architecture, more powerful than painting and sculpture, changes physical space even more radically; not only do we see a space which is not real but also we live and die in that second space."

Octavio Paz

                              The realized
is dung of the ground that feeds us, rots,
                              falls apart

           into the false,
displaying wounds of the pure
           urge, mounds
mulch for covetous burrowing thought.

           But from time's rot
it is toward another time we keep our root
           known.

                    Robert Duncan,
                    "Nor is the Past Pure"

Preface

Modern criticism in Canada has become a strikingly effective social instrument. It serves as a vehicle of political comment and social awareness. It seeks a central role in the development of national consciousness. It aspires to the attainment of cultural coherence. No one, I think, would quarrel with aims of this sort, particularly when they intend to serve the variety and richness of Canadian experience and more fairly represent the Canadian writer than earlier aesthetic criticism was able to. At the same time, writers remain traditionally uneasy allies of those in political struggle. Something in their craft draws them away from the public arena toward a place at once private and perilous or inward and rewarding. All literature addresses itself to this tension. But in a political time, the inward and ideal aspects of writing tend to diminish in fascination and power and come to seem for many no more than a prison of idealism, mere consciousness, or fantasy. So it is that one of the most difficult critical questions, the fictional nature of literary reality, is easily ignored or dismissed.

The essays collected here have been variously published or presented in seminars, and conferences, or as broadcasts, in part as a response to something that shows itself first, though its urgent form is literary, as a political question: the meaning of illusion in writing, the significance of living in words, of de-realizing the world, the fictional nature of the material itself. Or so it seems to me now. This isn't to say the essays are of one piece. They reflect a number of interests other than fantasy or fiction: the importance of a growing regionalism in Canada; the nature of the modern sensibility; the achievements of contemporary experimental writing. Moreover, they represent a response to the many requests I have received for comments on a number of subjects—modern Canadian writing in particular—and so they speak to interests larger than simply my own, something in the consciousness of many people over a period of years. They are reflections rather than arguments.

In selecting and arranging the essays, I have emphasized some interests over others and consciously tried to indicate a continuing concern. Both in design and emphasis, the collection follows from an earlier critical work, *Criticism: the Silent Speaking Words,* and provides in Canadian terms a version of theories of writing discussed there. But while I think the essays have some unity, I have not attempted to rewrite extensively nor to make them more aware than they originally were of the demands to which they respond.

Once, years ago, I remember a phrase of Yeats's possessed me: "In dreams begin responsibility." If there is one theme running through these essays, it would be that. I think there are no better commitments.
                                                                    Eli Mandel

Acknowledgements

Some of these essays have appeared elsewhere and are re-published here with thanks and acknowledgments to: *A Region of the Mind; Prairie Perspectives 2; Figures in a Ground; Identities; Indirections; Canadian Forum; Twentieth Century Literature; Rune; CBC; Impulse; The Malahat Review.* I am grateful as well to the audiences of those conferences and seminars where I was able to try out early versions of some papers here and to the large number of friends and colleagues who have read and commented on papers at various stages of writing, especially Dennis Lee who endured the earliest and roughest attempts. Bryan Flack and Glynnis Thomas read and corrected the ms and sought for lost footnotes, Connie Thompson assisted me in a final draft, and Evie Mandel's reading of the ms was invaluable. Without the assistance of Ann Mandel the work could not have been completed. So much of this is hers, it is difficult not to acknowledge her as a co-author, but her forthcoming book should separate my misjudgments from her achievements. Finally, acknowledgements as well to the Canada Council for grants in aid of research and to the Ontario Council of the Arts.

I
Reflections

The Poet
as
Critic

Steiner: "When he looks back, the critic sees a eunuch's shadow. Who would be a critic if he could be a writer? Who would hammer out the subtlest insight into Dostoevsky if he could weld an inch of the Karamazovs, or argue the poise of Lawrence if he could shape the free gust of life in *The Rainbow?*"[1]

Aside from whatever Steiner means by "a free gust of life," the passage raises a curious distinction that has haunted criticism at least since the romantic era, probably long before:

between the critical and the creative

between the secondary or derived and the primary or original

"The critic lives at second hand. He writes *about*. The poem, the novel, or the play must be given to him; criticism exists by the grace of other men's genius."[2] In *The Concept of Criticism,* Sparshott examines an argument very like this one: criticism must be criticism of.

It has always seemed to me peculiar to exclude from criticism in this way a large part of what has traditionally been thought of as criticism, the theorizing of Arnold, say, Blake's extravagant fancies, or Wilde's outrageous arguments in *The Decay of Lying* or *The Critic as Artist.* One of the characters in these dialogues declares himself to be astounded at the notion that a literary work should in any way be anything except a point of departure for the critic's own invention, and whatever else we might say about him, he seems, to me at least, more honest about his aims than most of our modern writers.

Sometimes it seems as if the critic-writer distinction is simply a disguised version of the form-energy tension within poetry itself, a means of talking about two opposing tendencies within poetry itself, a means of talking about two opposing tendencies within art, those variously described as imitation and design, or the mimetic and the abstract, the

11

symbolic and realistic, and so on. What happens, for example, when we begin to think of a work of criticism as a work of art? "By virtue of style, criticism can itself become literature. But usually this occurs only when the writer is acting as critic of his own work or as outrider to his own poetics, when the criticism of Coleridge is work in progress or that of T.S. Eliot propaganda. Is there anyone but Sainte-Beuve who belongs to literature purely as a critic? It is not criticism that makes the language live."[3]

I am not sure how or whether it follows that when the poet or writer is critic, his criticism will necessarily be literature or even literate. But what is evident is that there is a long tradition of critical writing by poets; one thinks of Sydney, Dryden, Wordsworth, Coleridge, Keats, in his letters certainly, Blake throughout his work, Wilde and Yeats, Pound, Eliot—Charles Olson, Creeley, and Duncan.

The sense in which their critical work can be thought of as secondary or derived puzzles me. The sense in which it involved them in a choice between creativity and critical work I find even more difficult to understand. For Steiner, criticism shows us what to reread, how to connect and what amidst our own chaotic lives is worth preserving: these tasks he finds secondary to the act of creation, though without them, he says, "creation itself may fall upon silence,"[4] I suppose in so far as a poem is an act of choice and discrimination and certainly some cry about whatever it is we love, it is a kind of criticism and hardly distinguishable from what the poet might want to say about it. The question of the relativity of his criticism, of his criticism as a defense of or rationalization for his own perceptions and poetry remains an even more difficult puzzle.

II MAKE IT NEW: A NEW THEORY OF CRITICISM?

"It is curious," says Pound, "that one should be asked to rewrite Sidney's *Defense of Poesy* in the year of grace 1913."[5] More curious, I suppose to rewrite it 40 years after Pound. But I think this is the question to which I am trying to get or to make clear: do we come to something new or do the poets, in their rationalization of their own work, simply restate perennial problems? Are we ever new men at all? Turning to the past Eliot and Pound rewrote literary history. It is still a surprise, to me at least, to look at the titles of the essays in the section on 'The Tradition' in Pound's *Literary Essays*, the volume for which Eliot wrote the introduction: Troubadors—their sorts and conditions; Arnaud Daniel; Cavalcanti; Hell; The Renaissance; Notes on Elizabethan Classicists; Translators of Greek; The Rev. G. Crabbe, LL.B., Irony, LaForgue and some Satire; The Hard and Soft in French Poetry; Swinburne versus his Biographers; Henry James; Remy de Gourmont.

Making it clear may mean making it new. I do think the past can be rewritten, and that to do so is not always wicked. But that still leaves this

12

question, for me the most important one: is there ever a new poetics? Allow me this personal example. I began to read George Steiner in 1967, about the time I had finished *An Idiot Joy* and when for a whole variety of reasons I was convinced I had written myself into a corner. Suddenly, with Steiner's incredibly eloquent essays in his book *Language and Silence*, broken bits of the past, lost perceptions, false starts, all began to fit together. At least the questions were clear. I knew now why James Agee's *Let Us Now Praise Famous Men* had seemed to me when I first read it a devastating work, one which was saying to me that we had to start all over again. And I knew that all the old terms were inappropriate, no longer adequate now. Like Steiner, though in a different context, Agee raised the one question which I had never once heard genuinely raised throughout all my years in the study of English Literature or anywhere among the writers whom I knew. The question had to do with the validity of the enterprise of art itself. The whole task of writing a book that in some profound and real way might reflect upon and illuminate in its wholeness and integrity the lives of human beings had, for Agee, become suspect, and he didn't hesitate to use in describing that task the word "obscene." There was something other than writing, other than words, that he wanted, the camera, perhaps, which he called "next to unassisted and weaponless consciousness, the central instrument of our time."[6] For Steiner, the question becomes displaced from creative to critical terms, from the dilemma of the writer to that of the critic, but the intent is the same. "There is some evidence that a trained persistent commitment to the life of the printed word, a capacity to identify deeply and critically with imaginary personages or sentiments, diminishes the immediacy, the hard edge of actual circumstance. We come to respond more acutely to literary sorrow than to the misery next door."[7] That can be put another way, in political terms: "the unprecedented ruin of humane values and hopes by political bestiality"[8] must be the starting point of any serious thought about literature and the place of literature in society; that argument, like Agee's argument, reminded me of Orwell too and Henry Miller, others who had argued peculiar connections of sensibility and politics, language and oppression.

I am still not prepared to say it is time for an auto-da-fé in Kingston, though I have been called a savage for even raising questions like these about the value of traditional literary forms or even of form itself. What I do think we have to address ourselves to is the kind of question Agee asks about form as a sort of murder, a question that since his time has been translated into a variety of terms, the most striking for myself being those presented in *Hope against Hope* and *The Savage God*, in Mandelstam's invincible conviction that all poets write their own deaths, in Alvarez's dark belief that the images we create may very well destroy us. Robert McDougall in an article called "A Perceptive Scenario for Cultural History" quotes Merleu-Ponty's dictum: "history is other people."[9] It is, he says, the world for others that fills and feeds my being. And yet, he admits, the poem is, if there, elsewhere as well. Where?

NOTES

1. George Steiner, *Language and Silence* (New York: Atheneum, 1967), p. 3.
2. *Ibid.*, p. 3.
3. *Ibid.*, p. 3.
4. *Ibid.*, p. 11.
5. Ezra Pound, *Literary Essays,* T.S. Eliot ed. (London: Faber & Faber, 1968), p. 41.
6. James Agee & Walker Evans, *Let Us Now Praise Famous Men* (New York: Ballantine, 1974), p. 11.
7. Steiner, p. 5.
8. *Ibid.*
9. R. McDougall, "A Perceptive Scenario for Cultural History", *The Literary Half-Yearly,* Anniah Gowda ed., Vol. XIII, No. 2, July 1972, p. 133.

The Poet
as
Liar

SOME COMMENTS ON SARTRE'S SAINT GENET

My subject is the poet as liar. It is an old subject, and I do not intend to
rehearse its long history. Nor do I want to involve myself in its logical
complications, the difficulties of propositional analysis, for example. It
may very well be that on this subject of lies all that is properly in our
province is that austere realm of silence revealed at the close of Wittgenstein's *Tractatus:* "There are, indeed, things that cannot be put into words."[1]
But one of the glories of literary criticism is its recklessness. And it seems
to me appropriate, then, to approach my subject through a reckless work.
I am going to talk about the form and argument of Sartre's *Saint Genet,*
and I am going to try to say in what sense the work might be thought of
as a hoax. It seems to me relevant, too, that Sartre argues Genet's poetry
is lies.

I

It is not difficult to think of literary works that present themselves as
hoaxes, or that in some way seem to be tainted, sometimes by the
author's disclaimer that he is the author of the book, sometimes by a
fantastic confusion of documentation and story, sometimes by a mocking tone that leaves us uneasy about the object of the faintly-concealed
laughter in the words we read. But the device which most peculiarly
dislocates our sense of what Marcus Klein calls "the author's authority,"
our sense of where the book stands in relation to us or to the world or to
its subject, is the device of reduplication, the power of a form to present
itself as an image of itself. Borges speaks of this self-referring power as
the Baroque, "that style which deliberately exhausts (or tries to exhaust)
its possibilities and borders on its own caricature."[2] And presumably it is
from Borges that John Barth takes his term "The Literature of Exhaustion"[3] to describe the hollow theatricality in what could be called "imita-

tion of style", the means by which, as Frye would have it, a writer chops holes in a rhetorical facade or breaks the story-teller's spell.[4] If we want examples of the contemporary baroque, certainly there are so many at hand that we might feel that in some way it is a peculiarly modern development. One thinks of the plays of Genet, the novels of Barth and Nabokov, the stories and parables of Borges, and especially those "metaphysical fantasies or mock heroics of logic"[5] that George Steiner concerns himself with: Valery's *Monsieur Teste*, Elias Canetti's *Auto-da-Fé*, Hermann Broch's *The Death of Virgil*, Péguy's "experiments in circular argument and incantation."[6] As these examples suggest, reduplication connects with the breaking-up of genre and the inter-mingling of modes of discourse. In contemporary jargon, we speak of the inter-media arts, but Jonathan Swift had no need of slides, tapes and graphics to create *The Tale of a Tub*. The question I am raising is whether certain kinds of literary criticism are not baroque forms, or to put it another and simpler way: is criticism too a form of fiction? Certainly, Swift's digressions on digressions lead us into a zany world that at least allows us to think of the critic as a character in his own story, though how he got there to begin with remains at best a puzzle.

I want to consider Sartre's *Saint Genet*, then, as a self-referring work about a self-referring figure. One might say that's an end of it. To have produced an argument for the little pimp as saint was, if a hoax, at least a neat trick, but to have done so at such a bloated and horrendous length was surely unpardonable. Still, one is uneasy. Sartre won't allow us the solace of cheap answers.

Take as an example the notion of the criminal saint. The first tempta-tion is to dismiss Sartre's as another version of the romantic diabolism of Beaudelaire, Rimbaud, Lautreamont, and Artaud. Or to link Genet, as Frye does, with De Sade's theory of natural society, "the cult of the holy sinner, the person who achieves an exceptional awareness, whether religious or aesthetic in character, from acts of cruelty, or, at least, brings about such an awareness in us."[7] No doubt, Sartre's feeling for Genet's diabolism *is* connected with the symboliste and surrealist traditions and the peculiar inversions in black romanticism. But, after all, literary history is only another evasion. If it is freedom you want to talk about— and that is Sartre's subject—you don't talk about 'literature.' "He who has read Kafka's *Metamorphosis* and can look into his mirror unflinching," says George Steiner, "may technically be able to read print, but is illiterate in the only sense that matters."[8]

> I have tried to do the following: to indicate the limit of psychoanalytical interpretation and Marxist explanation and to demonstrate that freedom alone can account for a person in his totality; to show this freedom at grips with destiny, crushed at first by its mischances, then turning upon them and digesting them little by little; to prove that genius is not a gift but the way out that one invents in desperate cases;

16

to learn the choice that a writer makes of himself, of his life and of the meaning of the universe, including even the formal characteristics of his style and composition, even the structure of his images and the particularity of his tastes; to review in detail the history of his liberation.[9]

Well, then, you may say, it's a moral question. We are either Christians or sophisticates, and so poor Genet cannot in either case shock us. For either view, the formalist or the Christian, Sartre has nothing but scorn:

> You have nothing to gain by putting yourself into a state of Christian charity, by loving him in advance and by accepting the pus of his books with the abnegation of the Saint who kisses the leper's lips. . . . Furthermore, do not take refuge in aestheticism; he will drive you from under cover. I know people who can read the coarsest passages without turning a hair: 'Those two gentlemen sleep together? And then they eat their excrement? And after that, one goes off to denounce the other? As if that mattered! It's *so* well written.' They stop at Genet's vocabulary so as not to enter his delirium.[10]

The alternative, then, as Sartre argues, is to *be* shocked. Don't put yourself above even that, not even if it means you must become like the critic M. Rousseaux. True, says Sartre, "this critic's incompetence is so sustained that one is tempted to maintain the opposite of everything he says. Yet that is the necessary test: if we want to win, we must be humble to the degree of becoming like unto M. Rousseaux."[11]

Sartre as M. Rousseaux. We begin to understand the proliferating form of the book: to save ourselves from delirium we are driven to linquistics, but that vocabulary crawls with vermin which will not allow us to dream the dream of the just and throws us back again to delirium. We dream that we are not dreaming in order that we may go on with our dream. As in a dream we find ourselves muttering portentous words that somehow tumble out like grotesque parodies of what we want them to say. Listen to Sartre's vocabulary as it tortures itself into what could only seem to Sartre himself a gross version of his characteristic language and a mockery of his means of reasoning: ". . . if, as Hegel says, there is a being of appearing as such, this being's reason for being and its destination are nothingness. If I think the moon is made of green cheese, this appearance has being only through what it denies: it is a negation of the moon by a non-being of cheese."[12]

Sartre's subject is language and freedom. And to talk of it he has got hold of a mirror-image, a self-referring form named Genet. Now, the really baffling point is that Genet, in so far as by this we mean his writing, is nothing. Genet freed himself by poetry. He was in prison. He wrote books, novels and poems, and because of these he was set free. But poetry is lies, appearance, hoax, fraud, nothingness; and if, as a general rule, you don't like to say that about poetry because of moral or philosophical scruples, you might as well put them aside. For, like Wilde's

DeProfundis, though with an added level of ironic awareness, Genet's novels are deliberate exercises in self-deception. Not, let it be noted, solipsistic arguments, but deliberate de-realizations of a sordid reality; and this being so, Sartre confronts his major problem, the problem which structures his book: how can *nothing* free us? Or to be more precise: how can an appearance which presents itself as an appearance be the vehicle of human freedom, of choice, of definition, of being, of good?

The criminal-prisoner who frees himself by poetry: that contains for Sartre the metaphor of man, the mystery of human action, the paradoxes of *being* that is good where ethics are an impossibility. And more mysteriously still, the fascination of opposites, splitting, identification, parody, the double. One of the basic devices of all fantastic literature, Borges tells us, is the double.[13] "Like the two youths in the fairy tale, their two horses, and their lilies" says Wittgenstein, "They are all in a certain sense one."[14] Is it so difficult to imagine the vertigo Sartre must have felt on seeing in the image of the criminal, himself? And in the literature of fantasy the language he as philosopher had laboured so long to forge? A world in which one thing could become another, not in fact, but in dream or myth, the self-creating fabulous world opened up in language. How baffling that these fabulous dislocations should be given to an obseqious, cringing, vulgar little man, the very picture of a humiliation so profound that we can do nothing but suspect it. Looking at Genet, Sartre looks at himself, and there sees the abyss, the hollowness, and all the words in whose vortex he must forever spin. So it is that Genet becomes for Sartre, first, myth, then object, and finally liar. It is only in these terms that he can understand that "Genet" means "patron saint of all the actors" and "comedian", a person "who shams or puts on an act." And it is to Genet then as myth, object, and liar we turn next, or if you like, to the meaning of parody, mockery, and silence, the language of literature as hoax.

II

Genet's life, according to Sartre, provides us with the dizzying spectacle of a man who creates himself through a series of transformations. The transformations are made necessary by the very condition of his existence. But it is that very necessity with which Genet must struggle. To put this another way, Genet is one of those for whom his own life is not a history but a myth. To say this is to invoke psychoanalytic notions, but if Sartre's account of the mythical Genet is psychoanalytic in its structure, it is something quite different in its language, and that seems to me the important point. This is the sort of thing we hear of the mythical Genet then: "An accident riveted him to a childhood memory and this memory became sacred. In his early childhood a liturgical drama was performed, a drama of which he was the officiant: he knew paradise and lost it, he was a child and was driven from his childhood."[15] Condemned to a drama of transformation, he lived in a memory that "condensed into a single mythical moment the contingencies and perpetual rebeginnings of an individual history."[16] Again, in Sartre's words, "Genet lives outside history, in parentheses. He no more cares about his individual adventure—which he contemptuously calls 'the anecdote'—than did an ancient Egyptian about his national history. . . . He is a man of repetition: the drab, slack time of his daily life—a *profane* life in which everything is permissible—is shot through with blazing hierophanies which restore to him his original passion."[17]

It is, in other words, not the analytic notion of fixation but the poetic one of the sacred that Sartre cares about. To think of oneself as a myth. Sartre describes how Genet crossed the border from Czechoslovakia to Poland. Crouching in the woods by a field of rye that lay on the border, he looked out at the puzzle nature seemed to offer him so blandly; and then under the most intense kind of excitement, he moved as a "heraldic character for whom a natural blazon had been formed: azure, field of gold, sun, forests."[18] He had discovered, Sartre says, that he was penetrating "less into a country than to the interior of an image,"[19] that he was intending to alienate himself from his own country, from all integrity. "I mean," he tells us, "that as a result of a certain frame of mind which is natural to enchantment . . . I was ready to act, not in accordance with the rules of morality but in accordance with certain laws of a fictional aesthetic. . . ."[20]

Genet as myth, then, is the Genet of pomp, display, glamour, magnification, the heraldic imagination. But we should not be misled. Genet is by no means all or only that which heraldry and ceremony might suggest. There is in him a coldness which we do well not to ignore.

"Genet is a child," says Sartre, "who has been convinced that he is, in his very depths, *Another than Self*. His life will henceforth be only the history of his attempts to perceive this Other in himself and to look it in the face. . . ."[21] In the jargon of analysis which Sartre now uses, "Genet slowly transforms himself into a stranger to himself";[22] that is, he progressively sets about "internalizing the sentence imposed by adults."[23] As mythic being, he is amid the "blazing hierophanies"[24] of a sacred world; but as object, he is a stranger to himself, in some terrible sense always absent. It would be beside the point to trace out here the complex play of self and other set up in a soul that feels its own absence. It is enough to observe that here begins that complex counterpointing of images, reflected and reflecting, so characteristic of Genet's work. The workings of the thief in quest of his stolen being are defined, says Sartre, by the mirror images of reflection-reflecting and of the reflection-reflected. Like Thomas Mann's Andre Leverkuhn, Genet in this guise is uncomprising intelligence, the awful lucidity of a consciousness aware of consciousness, to whom therefore all things are mocked by their own images.

But the mockery of reflection is further compounded, since the absent self which is its source is at the very same time the mythic being who lives a sacred timeless life. Genet's world is duplicitous at its very heart, at one and the same time a universe of analogies symbolizing everything and telling all, and a dance of reflection that tells us nothing at all.

> Prison offered me the first consolation, the first peace, the first friendly fellowship: I experienced them in the realm of foulness. . . . Prison offers the same sense of security to the convict as does a royal palace to a king's guest. They are the two buildings constructed with the most faith, those which give the greatest certainty of being what they are— which are what they are meant to be, and which they remain.[25]

And elsewhere, he develops the same themes: that the high and the low are linked in obscene ways, that everything has its own low and debased and gross parody, that to be conscious of oneself is to be aware only of one's absence from oneself but to be defined by others is only to be an object:

> The police of the various European countries inspired me with fear, just as they do any other thief. The French police moved me more through a kind of terror, the source of which was in my feeling of native and irrevocable guilt, than by the danger in which I was placed by my casual delinquencies. The world of the police, like the underworld, was a world which I would never enter.
>
> My lucidity (my awareness) kept me from drifting into that formless, moving, hazy universe, constantly self-creating, elementary and fabulous, of which the motorcycle police, with its attributes of force, is the delegation here below. That was what the French police, more than any other, meant to me. Perhaps because of its language, in which I discovered abysses. (It was no longer a social institution but a sacred power, acting directly on my soul and troubling me. Only the German police, in Hitler's time, succeeded in being both Police and Crime. This masterly synthesis of opposites, this block of truth, was frightful, charged with a magnetism that will continue to perturb us for a long, long time.)[26]

Viewing himself as myth and object, Genet then appeared as a creature of contradictions and paradoxes, and these can only be resolved or worked out in a mad dialectic which is the pattern of his life, a series of transformations or whirligigs that Sartre sketches out in his summary pages on "General Principles". For my purposes, it is not the mad process but the end product which is important, and that product, of course, is Genet's language, or rather Sartre's version of it. It is, I think, one of the most remarkable accounts of language as silence in the whole of literary criticism.

In one of his astonishing stories, Borges tells of a universe that is the imaginary creation of the literature of fantasy of a people who do not exist. One curious feature of the language spoken in this universe is that it has no nouns, but "the fact that no one believes in the reality of nouns" remarks Borges, "paradoxically causes their number to be unending."[27] This, I think, is as precise a description of Sartre's account of Genet's language as we are likely to get. Genet's language is determined by the distance he stands from the words we speak, and that distance is a product of the roles he must play. But each role, in turn, destroys the language of the previous role until at last, as poet, Genet knows the presence only of the word itself. His gift to us is a language so utterly destroyed that only he can live in it.

"Our words," says Sartre, "turn their backs to [Genet], designate absences, denote distance, name invisible things, refer to what is manifest to others and remains hidden from his eyes."[28] Condemned to silence because a culprit does not speak, he can only lie or deceive or steal words. He is a criminal, a passive homosexual, and a poet, and each of these roles gathers to it an increasingly complex dislocation or displacement of one language from the other. This is how Sartre puts it:

> He knows three languages: the common language, argot, the dialect of the queens; and he cannot speak any of them. What is worse, each of them interferes with the other two, challenges them, and finally destroys them. Whenever he speaks, he steals words, he violates them. He is a real thief and the signification of the statements he utters is imaginary, he lies; he is a fake bourgeois, a fake tough, a fake woman, he plays roles; the words are perhaps true, but the speaker is imaginary.[29]

The choice is pathetic: if the words are true, the speaker is imaginary; if the speaker is real, his words are lies. This is where Sartre's analysis of Genet's language finally leads: if you take Genet's words as truth, he doesn't exist; if you accept his existence, his words are lies. Always detached, ironic, lucid, Genet himself moves to the same conclusion as Sartre's and, like Sartre, plays off against each other both the pathos and a snickering threat in his words:

> Saintliness means turning pain to good account. It means forcing the devil to be God. It means obtaining the recognition of evil. For five years I have been writing books: I can say that I have done so with pleasure, but I have finished. Through writing I have attained what I was seeking. What will guide me, as something learned, is not what I have lived, but the tone in which I tell of it. Not the anecdotes, but the work of art. Not my life, but the interpretation of it.[30]

The conclusion seems to me inescapable. At the last, one might say, in his realm of foulness Genet was a purist precisely because he never once allowed himself to believe that style was anything but style, not life, not society, not psychology, and certainly not reality. This is, I think, what Sartre means when he tells us that Genet has "entered the readers' hearts and imparted to them his infernal lightness ... this void," that "he has restored *negativity* to them" and that "His victory is his being able 'to

21

be missing from himself and from everything': at the end of each poem he has said everything, and this was nothing."[31]

III

Sartre would have it that "[Genet] has not called anything into question,"[32] and there is a sense in which we have to agree. Everything, after all, depends on our remaining like M. Rousseaux. But I find it a vexing remark. Do we then simply account for Sartre and Genet as manifestations of bourgeois culture? The attractions of social criticism are powerful. One could argue, for example, as George Steiner does, that "the classic form and claims of the novel are inseparable from the bias of a middle-class humanistic culture" and that "their ruin is a common one."[33] And it may be precisely in the ruined novels of a writer like Genet that we can see what is left of our claims to reason and human knowledge. If the defining figure of humanism is the individual, then there he is, a wretched, locked-in ego endlessly reduplicating his dream of self. "Once History inhabits a crazy house" remarks Norman Mailer in his new work, *The Armies of the Night*, "egotism may be the last tool left to History."[34] But the argument is cheapened in just the way that Sartre has warned us not to cheapen it, that is, by taking it on Genet's terms. The more urgent question is surely the one about lies. What has all the fuss amounted to? That Genet is a liar? Surely there are more vital matters at hand. Nathan Scott remarks in a book about Samuel Beckett that all our transactions with the world are controlled by a deep and abiding faith that what we think and feel—and therefore say—about the world, has a chance of being metaphysically true.[35] That has a satisfying sound about it. But I think we might remind ourselves that Sartre and Genet are not the only liars in literature. Huck Finn certainly was one, if Mark Twain wasn't. Odysseus is even more of a liar than Huck, and if we are to believe John Barth, Meneleus is an even worse liar than Odysseus.

"His victory is his being able 'to be missing from himself and from everything'."[36] From one point of view, Genet's lightness is infernal. He is nothing, a void, emptiness, negativity, the very definition of the devil. There is another view possible. "The solution of the problem of life is seen in the vanishing of the problem" remarks Wittgenstein and he goes on "Is not this the reason why those who have found after a long period of doubt that the sense of life became clear to them have then been unable to say what constituted that sense?"[37] Sartre has written a book about nothing. Like all those others, Homer, Mark Twain, Shakespeare, who tell us their work is finally about itself, his work too is tautological. We can say, then, it is nothing. I prefer to think it is like the work of the philosophers in that imaginary world dreamed by a fictional people in Borges' story:

22

The metaphysicians of Tlon do not seek for the truth or even for verisimilitude, but rather for the astounding. They judge that metaphysics is a branch of fantastic literature.[38]

NOTES

1. Ludwig Wittgenstein, *Tractatus Logico-Philosophicus*, the German Text . . . with a new translation by D.F. Pears and B.F. McGuiness (London: Routledge and Kegan Paul, 1966), p. 151 (6.522).

2. Jorge Luis Borges, *Labyrinths* (New Directions, 1964), p. xxii.

3. John Barth, "Jorge Luis Borges: The Literature of Exhaustion", *Essays on Contemporary Literature*, R. Kostelanetz ed. (New York: Avon Books, 1964), p. 662.

4. Northrop Frye, *The Modern Century* (Toronto: Oxford University Press, 1967), p. 71.

5. George Steiner, *Language & Silence* (New York: Atheneum, 1967), p. 389.

6. *Ibid.,* p. 390.

7. Frye, p. 84.

8. Steiner, p. 11.

9. Jean Paul Sartre, *Saint Genet* (New York: George Braziller, 1963), p. 584.

10. *Ibid.,* p. 585.

11. *Ibid.,* p. 586.

12. *Ibid.,* p. 356.

13. Jorge Luis Borges, "Tales of the Fantastic", *Prism International* Vol. 8, No. 1, Summer, 1968. See also "Introduction" to Jorge Luis Borges, *Labyrinths* (New York: New Directions, 1964) by James E. Irby, p. xviii.

14. Wittgenstein, p. 39 (4.014).

15. Sartre, p. 1.

16. *Ibid.,* p. 5.

17. *Ibid.,* p. 5.

18. Jean Genet, *Thief's Journal* (New York: Grove Press, 1964), p. 48.

19. *Ibid.,* p. 49.

20. *Ibid.,* pp. 49-50.

21. Sartre. p. 35.

22. *Ibid.,* p. 37.

23. *Ibid.,* p. 37.

24. *Ibid.,* p. 5.

25. Genet, pp. 85-87.

26. *Ibid.,* p. 189.

27. Borges, *Labyrinths*, p. 9.

28. Sartre, p. 278.

29. *Ibid.,* pp. 293-294.

30. Genet, p. 205.

31. Sartre, pp. 567-568.

32. *Ibid.*, p. 567.

33. Steiner, p. 80.

34. N. Mailer, *The Armies of the Night* (New American Library, 1968), p. 54.

35. N.A. Scott, *Samuel Beckett* (New York: Hillary House, 1965).

36. Sartre, p. 568.

37. Wittgenstein, pp. 149-150 (6.521).

38. Borges, *Labyrinths,* p. 10.

Tennyson Through the Looking Glass

". . . most [American universities] can scarcely be considered as anything
other than a proving ground for the military establishment and industry.
. . . As arms factories nearly all the . . . multi-universities would have
staggered the imagination of Herr Krupp or Sir Basil Zaharoff. No
scheme for the destruction of the human race is wanting in their pro-
grams of 'research'. Social benefits do emerge, but mostly as by-products
. . . a miser's gold is meant to be counted but not otherwise enjoyed.

Some of the monies enlarged by government hand-outs naturally
trickles down to the professors of humanities, very few of whom are yet
of as much use in planning holocausts as are their scientific brother. It
must not be imagined, however, that these 'humanists' willingly consent
to be thrown back to instructing students . . . these second-class aca-
demics [are] as loath to contact students as their more highly advantaged
confrères in the hard sciences. They prefer, and indeed are forced, to
attempt to emulate the scientists. Often this takes the form of applying
the methods of science to the realms of discourse where these methods
obviously cannot apply. But what can the poor humanists do when they
are continuously challenged to justify their slots according to the test:
'what have you to contribute to General Motors?' "[1]

The words are John Wilkinson's from an address to the Centre for the
Study of Democratic Institutions, and I begin with them because I want
to elicit from them two attitudes that seem to me related to my purpose
in this paper: first, Wilkinson's rhetoric of apocalypse reminds me of that
young sociologist, who, in "Maud," preaches paradoxes of doom: love is
hate; war is peace; health is sickness; sanity is madness; and second, this
profound uncertainty about the nature and role of social institutions
goes along with uneasiness and confusion about the role of the critic.
Objectivity and disinterestedness, presumably the marks of both precision and fair-mindedness, begin to look like covert commitments to
values best left unexpressed or, at least, means of neutralizing the values

of humanism. "We apply methods of science to realms of discourse where those methods obviously cannot apply."[2]

The alternative to pseudo-science, of course, is not pseudo-art. If we follow Noam Chomsky—not always an easy thing to do—we might be willing to discover objectivity in our biases. Far from insisting that an explicit commitment to certain values should be avoided, Chomsky argues "Clear articulation of this commitment, which is never absent, is a prerequisite for objectivity."[3] Northrop Frye's critic inhabits a colder, more rarified atmosphere: some point where dialogue becomes dialectic and the subject itself takes over the person, freeing him, one supposes, from his wicked desire to cheat on the argument. I prefer Norman Brown's critic as interpreter, the psycho-pomp or conductor of souls, trickster, translater, shape-shifter, a counterfeit man. My reason is not, I trust, obscurantist, but simply that I agree with Brown when he remarks "we never say what we mean."[4] Oscar Wilde was surely right: critics, of necessity, are irrational, unfair, and insincere. Or, to put it another way, so far as my own limited reading of Tennyson's critics extends, I hear only the voices of contributions to General Motors. I mean, say, the conclusion to Buckley's *Tennyson, The Growth of a Poet:*

> . . . with all his own passion of the past, he intuited a lost order of values, a peace—both aesthetic and religious—untouched by the bewildering changefulness and relativity of the world. Behind the roar of the London street, he could imagine what once had been the stillness of the central sea, the elemental reality with which the spirit must once again come to terms. His response to the restless activity of his time enhanced rather than weakened his concern with the moment of insight and revelation. And his art, at its highest, transcending change, invested the transitory with meaning and purpose.[5]

It's really quite unexceptionable. But in other rooms other voices: this one, for example:

> Tragedy, sir. Deaths and disclosures, universal and particular, denouements both unexpected and inexorable, transvestite melodrama on all levels including the suggestive. We transport you into a world of intrigue and illusion . . . clowns, if you like, murderers. . . .[6]

"Only this?" You might ask, as indeed Guildenstern does ask of the player. "No enigma, no dignity, nothing classical, portentous, only this— a comic pornographer and a rabble of prostitutes." (*R and G,* p. 27)

To which, of course, the answer is: "Don't you see?! We're *actors*— we're the opposite of people!" (*R and G,* p. 63)

We could wonder why there is this reluctance to understand that Tennyson's actors are the opposite of people: the young poseur of "Locksley Hall," for example; the impossibly inflated spasmodic rhetorician of "Maud"; the posturing elocutionist of "The Vision of Sin"; the early second-rate mind playing with suicidal thoughts; the late blusterer of "Locksley Hall Revisited"; the multi-voiced orator tricked out as the hero

26

of "Ulysses"; those shadows receding into the late darkness of the "Idylls."

Yet there may be some justice on the side of those for whom none of these voices in Tennyson seems to belong properly in drama. 'Actor' doesn't seem to be precisely the word we want. As between science and acting, between scientist and actor, there is surely no doubt where Tennyson stands, however much he wanted his metaphors to be scientifically accurate, whatever that may mean. As between science and acting, criticism really has no choice. Tennyson's actors are strange ones, indeed. Insincere, of course; not people. And yet, do we want to say 'actor'? 'Player', perhaps, as the actors playing actors in *Hamlet* are called 'players'—or imposter or hypocrite or hysteric; something, at least, which suggests a tenous hold on the self, "unshadowable in words, /Themselves but shadows of a shadow-world."[7]

R.D. Laing employs Heidegger's contrast between two concepts of truth in order to point up the almost unlimited possibilities in the self's relation to its own acts, the gap between self and expression. It is not the scientific concept of truth as a correspondence "between the structure of a symbol system 'in the mind' and the structure of events 'in the world'" that is significant here. It is rather the pre-Socratic concept that lights up the shadowy aspects of self-concealment and ambiguity, that is the concept of truth as "literally that which is without secrecy" when indeed "in the light of this latter form of truth, one says a man is truthful or 'true to himself' if one feels he means what he says, or says what he means." It is the "untruth" that matters here, the lack "of final assurance that one can attribute correctly the other's relations of his actions." Laing lists those who are both exploiters and victims of duplicity: the liar (who deceives others without deceiving himself); the hysteric (who deceives himself before deceiving others); the actor (whose actions are not 'him'); the hypocrite, the imposter (who is absorbed in the role he plays).[8]

The appeal of a catalogue is symmetry: the liar (someone, say Lancelot, in the "Idylls") the hysteric: speaking in "Maud"; the actor: the voice of "In Memoriam"; the Prince of "The Princess"; the imposter, the hypocrite: Arthur, divine counterfeiter. But it is the "Lack of final assurance,"[9] not symmetry, that we should consider.

Confronted by a young hedonist singing lyrics of transience and satiation, the ancient sage recites those oracles about a dissolving self we hear elsewhere in Arthur's admonition to his knights for their mistaken asceticism in pursuit of vision, and hear again in the trance spelled out in the silent-speaking words of lyric 95 of "In Memoriam," and again in the account of the seizures suffered by the young man-woman hero of "The Princess." But if the prophetic word of the sage is, as he says, silent, its language is the same language of loss that informs not only the songs of "The Princess" but so early a poem as "Mariana":

The first gray streak of earliest summer-dawn,
The last long stripe of waning crimson gloom,
As if the late and early were but one—
A height, a broken grange, a grove, a flower
Had murmurs "Lost and gone and lost and gone"
A breath, a whisper—some divine farewell—
Desolate sweetness—far and far away—
What had he loved, what had he lost, the boy?

("The Ancient Sage", pp. 1355-6)
(ll. 220-227)

Unlike Jerome Buckley, the ancient sage remains properly silent on the answer to those questions, and instead moves on at once to the ultimate strangeness of language itself: words, themselves but shadows of a shadow-world. Beyond language, the sage asserts, there is something other than a counterfeit life, but it escapes the infinite regressions of name and word, the self's habitation.

Perhaps, then, there's something more than accident in what appears as an accidental link between Mann's *Dr. Faustus* and Tennyson's "The Princess." Shortly before we are told of the strange document which reveals Andre Leverhuhn's pact with the devil in Mann's *Faustus*, Leverhuhn has finished his musical version of Shakespeare's *Love's Labour's Lost*, a play, we note in passing, about affectation in language. Of Leverhuhn's musical, the somewhat finicky humanist who narrates *Faustus* remarks, "intellectual monkishness, a learned over refinement deeply contemptuous of life and nature both, which sees the barbaric precisely in life and nature, in directness, humanity, feeling."[10] In Tennyson's *Love's Labour's Lost, The Princess,* learned over-refinement expresses itself not only in trance, transvesticism, and gothic imagery of landscape and dream, but in the peculiar regressiveness of the Prince's affliction: he dreams himself the shadow of a dream. We're meant to take it that love heals these divisions; at least, so one reads the Prince's odd remark to Ida: "Accomplish thou my manhood"; but whatever resolutions we find in the story the framework quickly dissolves, both with the narrator's apology for a random scheme, and the feud between the "Mockers and the realists."

Presumably, a good deal of the bafflement felt by readers of "The Princess" has something to do with its Lewis Carrol people and Edward Lear landscape. For a long while it seemed to me that one really understood parody by reading the imitation as if it were the original. *Rosencrantz and Guildenstern are Dead,* indeed much of contemporary writing, from Borges to Barth, teaches us to go at the question the other way around: the way to understand parody is to read the original as if it were the imitation. Whether or not this means that only certain works can be parodied, it does remind us that "The Princess" is its own imitation, a multiplied mirror-image of itself. Self-parody. This is reflexiveness.

28

Role-playing, as in "The Princess," means playing parts, but we have to get clear what we mean by playing, and where that will take us. Hamlet, Act III, Scene II, advice to the players: ". . . anything so o'erdone is from the purpose of playing, whose end, both at the first and now, was and is, to hold, as 'twere, the mirror up to nature."

"I'll tell you all my ideas about looking-glass House" remarks Alice. "First, there's the room you can see through the glass—that's just the same as our drawing room, only the things go the other way. I can see all of it when I get upon a chair—all but the bit just behind the fireplace. . . . I do so wish I could see *that* bit! I want so much to know whether they've a fire in the winter: you never *can* tell, you know, unless our fire smokes, and then smoke comes up in that room too—but that may be only pretence, just to make it look as if they had a fire."[11]

That may be only pretence. You no longer can tell what anything is simply by looking at it: "for knowledge is of things we see" but "we cannot know" ("In Memoriam", Prologue, *Poems*, ll. 21-22, p. 863). Another possibility presents itself: a man can play at being an actor playing at being a man (Laing, 28) so that he ends up by *pretending* that the real room is real rather than by *perceiving* it as real. This double-pretence, described by Laing in *The Self and Others,* at once undercuts not only perception (the world turning into an appearance) but will and freedom as well.

A sinister, because scarcely noticed, version of the double-pretence is "In Memoriam." To deny a sorrow which he feels both proves and denies his love, the poet is led to affirm its truth in its lies and its reality in its appearance. It must be at one and the same time true and false, something he means and does not mean:

> Come, Time and teach me, many years,
>   I do not suffer in a dream
> For now so strange do these things seem
>   Mine eyes have leisure for their tears.
>   ("In Memoriam", 13, ll. 13-16, p. 876)

But if that plea sounds hollow, what are we to make of the later admission, surely one of the most devastating in all poetry; it comes in lyric 125 of "In Memoriam": "Love but played with gracious lies, / Because he felt so fixed in truth." What Tennyson is saying is that his pretence of sorrow was the reality of his sorrow. Nor has he shirked the consequence: the only way in which he can affirm the reality of a derealized world is to pretend: regressively, it is the dream of a dreamer that is reality, and this is so whether we take as Tennyson's "resolution" the trance of lyric 95, a seeming or appearance of a trance, or the "idea" of Hallam as a type of humanity's potential, a notion revealed and confirmed in the dream vision of lyric 103, or the more explicit version of dream-reality in lyric 123:

There rolls the deep where grew the tree.
  O earth, what changes hast thou seen!
There where the long street roars, hath been
The stillness of the central sea.

The hills are shadows, and they flow
  From form to form, and nothing stands;
They melt like mist, the solid lands,
  Like clouds they shape themselves and go.

But in my spirit will I dwell
  And dream my dream and hold it true;
For though my lips may breathe adieu,
  I cannot think the thing farewell.

As Stoppard would say, "there are precedents for mystical encounters."
(R and G, p. 21)

> A man breaking his journey between one place and another at a third
> place of no name, character, population, or significance, sees a unicorn
> cross his path and disappear. That in itself is startling, but there are
> precedents for mystical encounters of various kinds, or to be less ex-
> treme, a choice of persuasions to put it down to fancy; until—"My
> God," says a second man, "I must be dreaming, I thought I saw a uni-
> corn." At which point, a dimension is added that makes the experience
> as a alarming as it will ever be. A third witness, you understand, adds
> no further dimension but only spread it out thinner, and a fourth thin-
> ner still, and the more witnesses there are the thinner it gets and the
> more reasonable it becomes until it is as thin as reality, the name we
> give to common experience. . . . "Look, look!" recites the crowd, "a
> horse with an arrow in its forehead! It must have been mistaken for a
> deer!" (R and G, p. 21)

Metaphysically, there's some force to McLuhan's argument that Tennyson's position is either gnostic or manichaean: existence is demonic, a
darkness which absorbs the light or gleam of creativity, and yet the *only*
means by which creativity might find expression. Psychologically, the
double-pretence seems to be connected with the attitude Mary McCarthy
notes in a writer quite unlike Tennyson: "It is as though . . . he wished to
be acted *upon*, rather than to act, that is, to follow the line of least
resistance and see where it led—a quite common impulse in a writer,
based on a mystical feeling that the will is evil."[12]

But as with Rosencrantz and Guildenstern, both of whom attempt to
locate the metaphysics of the play they are acting, in order to understand
who they are and whether they are free, form itself becomes or creates
its own metaphysic, the principles of which we are only just now beginning to rediscover:

> A Chinaman of the T'ang Dynasty—and, by which definition, a philos-
> opher—dreamed he was a butterfly, and from that moment he was
> never quite sure that he was not a butterfly dreaming it was a Chinese
> philosopher. (R and G, p. 60)

The same sort of puzzle appears in *A Midsummer Night's Dream* when Hippolyta wonders how four people could all have the same dream, or when she tells Theseus he is imagining the actors who, Theseus replies, imagine themselves. It seems to be something like a law that certain images (those Borges would say we cannot invent but only discover) not only reduplicate themselves but create a world in their own pattern. "The practice of literature," says Borges, "sometimes fosters the ambition to construct an absolute book, a book of books that includes all the others like a Platonic archetype."[13] Whatever principle of identity is at work here, it is obvious enough that for Tennyson the poetic character and his world mirror one another. At one extreme, we would have to place the madman of *Maud* whose theatrics reflects a mad society; at the other, Arthur, whose Camelot is an astonishing projection of his own ambiguities.

When Gareth and his men approach Camelot for the first time, they reel back in fright at what they see, and Gareth challenges Merlin for some explanation:

> these, my men,
> (Your city moved so weirdly in the mist)
> Doubt if the King be King at all, or come
> From Fairyland; and whether this be built
> By magic, and by fairy Kings and Queens;
> Or whether there be any city at all,
> Or all a vision. . . . ("Gareth and Lynette", ll. 240-246, p. 1490)

But Merlin's answer is all riddling:

> for there is nothing in it as it seems
> Saving the King; though some there be that hold
> The King a shadow, and the city real:
> Yet take thou heed of him, for, so thou pass
> Beneath this archway, then wilt thou become
> A thrall to his enchantments, for the King
> Will bind thee by such vows, as is a shame
> A man should not be bound by, yet the which
> No man can keep; but, so thou dread to swear,
> Pass not beneath this gateway, but abide
> Without, among the cattle of the field.
> For an ye heard a music, like enow
> They are building still, seeing the city is built
> To music, therefore never built at all,
> And therefore built for ever. ("Gareth and Lynette", ll. 260-273,
> p. 1491)

The notion of a giant form viewed close at hand as a multitude and at a distance as one man will be familiar to readers of Blake, and in Blake they will find a single form named Albion who not only contains all the counties of England but who, in Frye's words, attempts "to emerge from time into eternity as one Man who is also a City of God."[14] Something of Arthur's ambiguity may be connected with the fact that, in such imagery, characteristically, body and city are identified: "The true Ark of God" remarks Frye, "is the human body, as Jesus implied when he identified his body with the temple."[15] "As in dreams" remarks Norman O. Brown, "the whole landscape is made out of the dreamer's body."[16]

Borges calls the inter-play of dream and waking one of the basic devices of fantasy, and one would like to think he would read Tennyson as a poet of wonder and astonishment, an industrious *monstorum artifex*,[17] as he says of Chesterton, a contriver of nightmares. A link suggests itself with Poe and Baudelaire, not only in their cultivation of extreme states of mind but in their deliberate creation of a world of terror. There is something in Tennyson, to use Borge's words, "secret, and blind, and central."[18] It accounts for the curious metaphors, the hands and houses of "In Memoriam", the shadowless perspective of eternity, the garden of sleeping souls; the king who is a city; it accounts for his odd evasiveness; the odd tonalities in a poet who more than any other English poet had mastered the sound values of his language; above all, it accounts for the darkness that led him to end his greatest poem in a murderous landscape of slain men and the wailing of those shadowy women in whose hands the dead king lies.

I am not trying to resurrect Nicolson's Tennyson, that morbid lyricist whose talent lay in lyrics of Lancashire twilights and limestone. I am insisting on the profound evasiveness, even the deceit and duplicity, of his poetic world, at least so far as that world is defined by what I take to be his major poems: "The Princess", "Maud", "In Memoriam", "The Idylls of the King." These seem to me essentially theatrical pieces, a poetry of loss.

> Our names shouted in a certain dawn . . . a message . . . a summons. . . . There must have been a moment, at the beginning, where we could have said—no. But somehow we missed it. (*R and G*, p. 125)

> 'Lost and gone and lost and gone!'
> A breath, a whisper—some divine farewell—
> Desolate sweetness—far and far away—
> What had he loved, what had he lost, the boy? ("The Ancient Sage", pp. 1355-1356)

There is a footnote—or an aside—or a player's speech to the audience.

"Let us keep things in proportion. Assume, if you like, that they're going to kill him. Well, he is a man, he is mortal, death comes to us all etcetera, and consequently he would have died anyway, sooner or later. Or to look at it from the social point of view—he's just one man among many, the loss would be well within reason and convenience. And then again, what is so terrible about death? As Socrates so philosophically put it, since we don't know what death is, it is illogical to fear it. It might be . . . very nice. Certainly it is a release from the burden of life, and for the godly, a haven and a reward. Or to look at it another way—we are little men, we don't know the ins and the outs of the matter, there are wheels within wheels, etcetera—it would be presumptuous of us to interfere with the designs of fate or even of kings. All in all, I think we'd be well advised to leave well alone. Tie up the letter—there—neatly—like that— They won't notice the broken seal, assuming you were in character." (*R and G*, p. 110)

But why Stoppard's *Rosencrantz and Guildenstern*? Why not *Hamlet*? or *Love's Labour's Lost*? Again, accident, accidental resemblance, fortuitous conjunction may be all we have to go on. But it seems worth noting that much of what is central to Tennyson—loss that is gain; an absence that is a presence; a voice that is silence; the end of words or language—may remind us of the new aesthetic of silence that forms contemporary literature and that George Steiner, for one, sees in the philosophical speculations of Wittgenstein, the drama of Beckett, and the music of John Cage. Pretence: that which happens in the part of the looking glass world we cannot see; secrecy, evasion, an absence. We may very well be left only with a question or questions: protesting their role, the players affirm its necessity; having once chosen to play at acting real, is it possible to be free?

> We can move, of course, change direction, rattle about, but our movement is contained within a larger one that carries us along as inexorably as the wind and current. . . . Who are we that so much should converge on our little deaths? . . . it is not enough. To be told so little— to such an end—and still, finally, to be denied an explanation. . . . (*R and G*, p. 122)

Tennyson affirms the freedom of will and the validity of the self; his ethical position is unequivocal; a commitment to action and social responsibility, sanctioned by God and faith. But then Rosencrantz and Guildenstern meant well too.

NOTES

1. J. Wilkinson, *"The Civilization of Dialogue"*, *A Centre Occasional Paper*, Centre for the Study of Democratic Institutions, Vol. III, No. 1, Dec. 1968, p. 6.

2. *Ibid.*

3. N. Chomsky, "Objectivity and Scholarship", *American Power and the New Mandarins* (New York: Pantheon Books, 1967), pp. 23-159.

4. Norman O. Brown, "On Interpretation", *CBC "Ideas" Tape* (Toronto: CBC, 1970 (?)).

5. J.H. Buckley, *Tennyson: The Growth of a Poet* (Boston: Houghton Mifflen, 1965), pp. 255-256.

6. Tom Stoppard, *Rosencrantz & Guildenstern Are Dead* (New York: Grove Press, 1967), p. 23.

7. Alfred Lord Tennyson, "The Ancient Sage", *The Poems of* . . . (London: Longman's, 1969), p. 1356, ll. 238-239.

8. R.D. Laing, *The Self & Others* (London: Tavistock Public, 1961), pp. 120-121.

9. *Ibid.*

10. Thomas Mann, *Doctor Faustus* (New York: Knopf, 1948), p. 217.

11. Lewis Carroll, *The Annotated Alice* (Great Britain: Penguin Books, 1970), pp. 180-181.

12. Mary McCarthy.

13. Jorge Luis Borges, *Other Inquisitions 1937-1952* (New York: Simon and Schuster, 1968), p. 66.

14. Northrop Frye, *Fearful Symmetry* (Princeton University Press, 1947), p. 248.

15. *Ibid.,* p. 368.

16. Norman O. Brown, *Love's Body* (New York: Random House, 1966), p. 49.

17. Borges, p. 83.

18. *Ibid.*

The Language
of
Silence

The subject—silence—has an historical dimension, a political dimension, an aesthetic dimension. Obviously, one has other choices: a religious choice, for example, to speak about God's silence or his language; or a psychological choice, to speak of the analyst's silence. But there are imperatives of occasion. Today, or so George Steiner insists, the question of silence is different from the question Job asked himself and flung to the universe: "I cry out unto thee and thou dost not answer me."[1] In any event, we receive no answer. No voice. An exceptional rigour imposes itself on us. We might want to say, "Look now, anything goes. There are no rules about what we can say or need not say. Given a topic like 'silence', we now can say anything or nothing at all." All possibilities remain open. Not to mention the paradoxes about the silence of noise or the speaking picture or the poetry in the spaces *between* the words. But I am suggesting that one should avoid this temptation. The very *openness* of the subject asks, first of all at least, that its boundaries or limits be drawn with a strictness one might not want elsewhere.

The boundaries for our time, I would suggest, are those to which Steiner draws our attention, those Wittgenstein drew around the subject in the closing sections of the *Tractatus*.[2] What I cannot talk about cannot be put into words. Therefore my silence about that is a silence that speaks of manifest things. What is shown forth, evident, but also—if we trust the etymology of *manifest*—what is hostile, offensive; as a manifesto declares its hostility and offends. But my boundaries are not what cannot be said but rather what can be, that is, the historical, political, and aesthetic dimensions of silence, all shadowed, doubtful areas, and all to be viewed as questions.

". . . imagine yourself gazing in a concave mirror, where your image vanishes to infinity and then appears beside you. In exactly the same way, when self-consciousness has passed from you and made its way into the infinite distances, grace is acquired, and this quality of grace, as it appears in the human body, possesses the greatest purity when there is either no self-consciousness or else an infinite self-consciousness: *either the mechanical doll or the god. . . .* The doll and the god between them have the mastery of art. There is perversity in the dance. Sometimes the doll appears, sometimes the god; then they vanish, and all we see is the crass human body attempting to imitate art."[3]

So Robert Payne comments in his meditation on the nature of the puppet-dance in his study of Chaplin. Payne sees Chaplin's art of mime, the silent dance, as a kind of transcendence. Curiously, his remarks call to mind an image from Rilke's *Duino Elegies,* one that Susan Sontag discusses:

"A prerequisite of 'emptying out' is to be able to perceive what one is 'full of', what words and mechanical gestures one is stuffed with, like a doll; only then, in polar confrontation with the doll, does the 'angel' appear, a figure representing an equally inhuman though 'higher' possibility, that of an entirely unmediated, trans-linguistic apprehension. Neither doll nor angel, human beings remain situated within the kingdom of language."[4]

The myth that language is a fall into consciousness, along with its corollary, the myth of transcendence, of going beyond language or through language to silence, is Oriental. Or so George Steiner argues in one of the major studies of the order of words.[5] The myth of transcendence does appear in Western thought, in the Trappists, in the Stylites, and the Desert Fathers, in Saint John of the Cross, but these, Steiner argues, are anomalies, departures from the main stream of classic western feeling. Western civilization is essentially verbal in character. It owes its character to its Greek-Judaic inheritance, to the Hebrews, people of the Book, to the Apostle who tells us that in the beginning was the Word, to the primacy of the word in Greek thought. So to Western man silence is terror. It is the void, the abyss. The mute man, says Steiner, bears a terrible scar. Tearing out of the tongue is one of the earliest, most horrible of punishments. And yet for the past three hundred years what we have witnessed in the west is a retreat from the word. For Steiner, the history of silence is primarily the history of a disastrous diminishing of verbal language, a calamitous descent or fall from the essential literacy of civilization. He calls this fall the crisis of rational, humane values.[6]

It is important that two matters be made clear at this point: the first is Steiner's unequivocal insistence that verbal language itself is the vehicle of reason: "The classic and the Christian sense of the world strive to order reality within the governance of language. Literature, philosophy, theology, law, the arts of history, are endeavours to enclose within the bounds of rational discourse the sum of human experience, its recorded past, its present condition and future expectation."[7] At certain privileged moments, to be sure, we go beyond speech. Language is bounded. It has its limits: a certain mute radiance or illumination beyond words; a rhythmic source in sound itself that translates itself into music, not words. We reach toward these in the most intense and perhaps the most private moments of our experience. But let us not be mistaken. Beyond the limits of language we find something queer. Since it is beyond reason, beyond articulation, beyond the clarity of discourse, it is not to be trusted. Its unseen face may be that of a god, but more likely a beast. And so, the second matter: what is distinctively human is speech. Says Steiner: "That articulate speech should be the line dividing man from the myriad forms of animate being, that speech should define man's singular eminence above the silence of the plant and the grunt of the beast—stronger, more cunning, longer of life than he—is classic doctrine well before Artistotle. . . . Possessed of speech, possessed by it, the word having chosen the grossness and infirmity of man's condition for its own compelling life, the human person has broken free from the great silence of matter. Or, to use Ibsen's image: struck with the hammer, the insensate ore has begun to sing."[8]

Once given Steiner's position, what follows has a certain inevitability, symmetry, and in his version, the eloquence of a great lament for the fall of a city and the arrival of the barbarians within its walls. The argument is relatively simple: the authority of literate humanism over experience diminishes as another, silent language replace its verbalism. Mathematical symbol replaces word. With the formulation of highly analytical structures, mathematics broke free of its empirical base and became a language in its own right, a language moreover whose history *"is one of progressive untranslatability,"* as Steiner puts it.[9] And it is a language whose authority over reality is greater than that of the word. The silent speech of mathematics. Once its authority makes itself felt, history, economics, the social sciences, even philosophy, all tumble, like far-eastern kingdoms going under one by one according to the domino theory of the masters of the Pentagon. Fleeing from language to mock-science, the humanities turn inside-out, until art and poetry too give up the last fortress of the word, and uncreating darkness covers all. Only the scratching of the mathematician's chalk on his blackboard now can be heard, and outside the schoolroom, the grunts and yowls of those to whom speech could scarcely matter less.

For all its eloquence, Steiner's account of the retreat from the word is grossly misleading. His position, traditional and elitist, allows only for the narrowest possible definition of literacy, the language of the Cambridge gentleman. Cut free of its moorings in reason, modern art, he would say, is brutalized and brutalizing. Modern language is debased because, in his words, "the image of the world is receding from the communicative grasp of the word."[10] Without its roots in tradition, modern society is hopelessly vulgar, a monkey-hutch of babblers and baboons. So he asks "What save half-truths, gross simplifications, or trivia can, in fact, be communicated to that semi-literate mass audience which popular democracy has summoned into the market place?"[11] The answer, of course, is that, historically, Steiner's question makes no sense at all: there is no evidence for the notion that art is linked only to the tastes and preferences of a minority group. But equally he is wrong in his estimate of the extent and effect of the retreat from the word. Literacy, in the sense of the authority of the book, may well have been under-mined by technological developments in communication devices, but that these developments herald the end of speech seems unduly pessi-mistic. To evoke standards here is the typical evasion. Not less speech, but bad speech. But whose standards are being invoked? Linguistically, the notion that language decays is highly suspect. And as for the sup-posed impoverishment of words because their perceptual function has been taken over by mathematics, the point makes sense only if words truly are vehicles of reason.

" 'To perish by silence': that civilization on which Apollo looks no more will not long endure," says Steiner.[12] Lovely words, and true enough. But their meaning and effect depend entirely on what one thinks of civilization itself and therefore of literacy. One of the major impulses of the modern era has been a radical critique of civilization, particularly of its Apollonian order and the forms it imposes. In the work of Schopen-hauer, Nietzsche, Freud, Frazer, it is not Apollo, but Dionysius whose voice we hear. What does the god of light and form mean to the apostles of violence? To Franz Fanon, say, to the wretched of the earth, or the young romantic anarchists whose explicit target, the university, is the temple of reason, lucidity, order, and illumination, Apollo's world? One can admire Steiner's courageous refusal to yield to inhumanity and brutality just as one can admire Orwell's thorny individualism; but pro-phetic though Orwell was and profound as Steiner is on the nature of totalitarianism, neither seems aware of the contradictions in his posi-tion. Orwell's cure for Newspeak was ironically to substitute an impov-erished language rather like the languages Swift was fond of imagining for his benevolently tyrannical kingdoms. In the same way, Steiner's humanism makes beasts of all his contemporaries. Plainly, his theme is the inhumanity of the humanities. Plainly, he implicates high literacy, literate civilization, in the barbarism of our time, the temptations, as he puts it, of the inhuman. But just to the degree that literate civilization itself is the violence and inhumanity it condemns, to that very degree it offers no solution to violence or barbarism. Steiner, like Orwell, would have it that the political dimensions of silence are the writer's refusal to use words that have been debased by propaganda, by political lies, by the horrible accounting-jargon of the death camps. And it is true that one reason for the strategy of silence among contemporary writers is poli-tical. But that strategy, that silence, is equally a refusal and an evasion. It involves turning one's back on the death camps. It involves the delicate

38

reticence of the literate man who will not deign to speak the language of one lower than himself. And for that very reason, it confirms and continues to be implicated in what it abhors.

A reticent language, one that will not say certain words because they have been spoiled or are wicked or debased, simply confirms the possibility of bestiality. The reasonable man creates his own image, the beast of Belsen.

From the point of view of a Dionysian, like Norman O. Brown, the reticence of the ego *means* violence: "to have a self is to have enemies, and to be a self is to be at war (the war of every man against every man)."[13] To break the walls of self is not to seek the reticence of reason nor the silence of not-speaking, but another silence:

"We stumble on the truth. The truth is always scandalous, a stumbling block; truth is where we stumble or fall. . . . The truth is in the error. . . . The original mistake. . . . The God of Delphi, who always spoke the truth, never gave a straight answer. . . . He always spoke in riddles, in parables; ambiguities . . . that hearing they might hear and not understand."[14]

And so we come upon a different, a new sense of silence, as Brown tells us: "To recover the world of silence, of symbolism, is to recover the human body. 'A subterranean passage between mind and body underlies all analogy.' The true meanings of words are bodily meanings, carnal knowledge; and the bodily meanings are the unspoken meanings. What is always speaking silently is the body."[15]

To put it another way: the silence of language Brown speaks of is neither a retreat from language because of some imputed loss of authority in words, nor the polite restraint of one who would not say what has been tainted. It is a profound silence within words themselves, a mystery and a mystification, the word as body. Brown seeks to recover the physicality of language, to see and know words as signs and wonders and as things. He seeks something more, to transform the political problem of silence into an aesthetic eschatology: "The revolution, the revelation, the apocalypse is vision; which pronounces a last judgment; and brings about the end. Aphorism is the form of last judgments; sentences."[16]

We have then two major accounts of silence, a political one which takes it that silence is a retreat from the word and therefore from civilization itself; and an aesthetic one which takes it that silence reveals the true form of language and the one possibility of a revolution in consciousness that could literally transform the human body. In other words, both Steiner and Brown take it that repression is the clue to understanding civilization, though one would build only upon repression while the other would seek to destroy it or at least to understand the void, the abyss, the emptiness that is the repressed world:

"To restore to words their full significance . . . is to reduce them to nonsense, to get nonsense or nothingness or silence back into words; to transcend the antinomy of sense and nonsense, silence and speech. It is a destruction of ordinary language, a victory over the reality-principle; a victory for the god Dionysius; playing with fire, or madness; or speaking with tongues; the dialect of God is solecism."[17]

Something of the meaning of Brown's cryptic eschatology comes clear in Susan Sontag's discussion of the aesthetics of silence, though she of course moves across a far wider range of possibilities than I suggest here. Distinguishing between art as an expression of human consciousness and art as the antidote to consciousness or as expressing the mind's capacity for self-estrangement, she plays out the ironies and paradoxes involved.

The seriousness of contemporary art is its refusal to be serious. As a spiritual project, art is gratuitous, and therefore a denial of its spirituality or transcendence; it follows it has to be overthrown, and as Miss Sontag says the "new element [that] enters the individual art work and becomes constitutive of it [is] the appeal . . . for its own abolition."[18] A parallel she draws is with the paradoxes involved "in attaining an absolute state of being described by the great religious mystics": "the activity of the mystic must end in a *via negativa*, a theology of God's absence, a craving for the cloud of unknowing beyond knowledge and for the silence beyond speech."[19]

To find fullness where there is only emptiness; to see everything where there is nothing; to assert by denying; to see how far, to what incredible point of exactness, it is possible to carry the project of renunciation in order still to affirm, it is on these paradoxes and with this ruthlessness that contemporary art exists. Or to put it as Miss Sontag does:

> Silence is a strategy for the transvaluation of art, art itself being the herald of an anticipated radical transvaluation of human values. . . .
>
> Silence is a prophecy, one which the artist's actions can be understood as attempting both to fulfill and to reverse.
>
> As language points to its own transcendence in silence, silence points to its own transcendence—to a speech beyond silence.[20]

I think, to put the point as simply as possible without doing violence to it, she is arguing that silence has become a framing device in contemporary writing, that is, a means of focusing attention, of enabling us to see what we have not seen before. The reasons for this choice are not at all clear though they do connect in some way with the collapse of humane values and with the artist's resolute refusal to see easy solutions. It is not easy to use words that are empty. It is not easy to speak to the void or to the unanswering abyss. It is not easy to construct objects meant to affirm your spirituality that at once deny it. The miracle is that anyone writes at all. Or perhaps rather that through strategies of silence the writer has found ways to intensify the word: And so Sontag says,

"A coquetish, even cheerful nihilism. One recognizes the imperative of silence, but goes on speaking anyway. Discovering that one has nothing to say, one seeks a way to say *that*."[21]

A silent poem is finally unacceptable. It violates language. It speaks of an end to words. And yet it offers a beginning. It is the most profound gesture of contempt and yet it is the greatest honour we pay to language, to another's words, listening to them. But it pays honour to the world, too, redeeming it, because it waits upon "thing", plant or beast, to hear them, or to hear the deep rhythms of the universe, or to hear only, as John Cage heard in a place of silence, the sound of one's own blood coursing through one's veins and one's own heart beating.

NOTES

1. George Steiner, *Language and Silence* (New York: Atheneum, 1967).

2. *Ibid.*, p. 21.

   Ludwig Wittgenstein, *Tractatus Logico-Philosophicus*, the German text . . . with a new Translation by D.F. Pears and B.F. McGuiness. (London: Routledge and Kegan Paul, 1966), pp. 147-149.

3. Robert Payne, *Charlie Chaplin*. (New York: Ace Books Inc., 1962), p. 40.

4. Susan Sontag, *Styles of Radical Will*. (New York: Farrar, Straus and Giroux, 1969), p. 24.

5. Steiner, pp. 12-13.

6. *Ibid.*, esp. "The Retreat from the Word", *passim*.

7. *Ibid.*, pp. 13-14.

8. *Ibid.*, p. 36.

9. *Ibid.*, p. 14, Steiner's italics.

10. *Ibid.*

11. *Ibid.*, p. 26.

12. *Ibid.*, p. 35.

13. Norman O. Brown, *Love's Body* (New York: Random House, 1966), p. 149.

14. *Ibid.*, pp. 243-245.

15. *Ibid.*, p. 265.

16. *Ibid.*, p. 232.

17. *Ibid.*, pp. 258-259.

18. Sontag, p. 5.

19. *Ibid.*, pp. 4-5.

20. *Ibid.*, p. 18.

21. *Ibid.*, p. 12.

II
Writing West

Images
of
Prairie Man

A subject like "images of prairie man" involves a number of difficult questions. At the simplest and most obvious level, presumably one accepts some kind of pluralistic approach, and then merely lists, in as interesting a way as possible, all those works which have concerned themselves with the prairies or the plains area; this kind of listing, we know, suggests, if nothing else, at least the variety and range of articulate response to an environment, all the way, for example, from that extraordinary blend of history, legend, and reminiscence, Wallace Stegner's *Wolf Willow*, to a curious and perhaps justly uncelebrated pamphlet in the Social Credit Board Education Series, *Alice in Blunderland*. But pluralism, like interdisciplinary conferences, raises its own questions: the question of coherence and unity, for example. What, if anything, do we find in common, in, say the Manitoba of Martha Ostenso, of Frederick Philip Grove, of Gabrielle Roy, of Adele Wiseman, and John Marlyn? Or what mysterious links can we discover between the radical metaphors of Wilfred Watson's *Friday's Child* and the descriptive impressionism of Anne Marriot's *The Wind Our Enemy*? We might, of course, content ourselves with observing that, by definition, unique responses remain unique, but then my subject simply disappears. An infinite variety of unique responses can never add up to the commonality implied by "prairie man." Indeed, the kind of articulation, patterning, and signification we mean by the term "image" suggests that we are looking for impressions and responses that have been raised into the order of thought. If we mean seriously to talk about images of prairie man, we are in fact concerned with prairie art and prairie literature, and we believe that somehow, as art and literature, they can be distinguished from other forms of art and literature.

Let me suggest the extreme limits of our discussion here: one limit seems to me to be what I would call the sociological one; the other, mythical. The sociological sees literature and art as reflections of (or interactions with) environment. Everyone knows Paul Hiebert's superb parody of such an approach to literature. Of Sarah Binks, the sweet songstress of Saskatchewan, he remarks, "Unschooled, but unspoiled, this simple country girl has captured in her net of poesy the flatness of that great province."[1] That approach, after all, is not so very different from W.D. Lighthall's in his Introduction to *Songs of the Great Dominion*, an 1889 anthology of Canadian Poetry. Lighthall was convinced his poets, like Sarah, sounded the depths of geography and history: "Through them, taken all together, you may catch something of great Niagara falling, of brown rivers rushing with foam, of the crack of the rifle in the haunts of the moose and caribou, the lament of vanishing races singing their death-song as they are swept on to the cataract of oblivion. . . ." Lighthall, by the way, was a great enthusiast who loved to celebrate Canada in tones worthy of any Board of Trade Chairman: "her four-thousand-mile panorama of noble rivers," he exclaims, "[her] wild forests, ocean-like prairies; her towering snow-capped Rockies. . . . She has by far the richest extent of fisheries, forests, wheat lands, and fur regions in the world; some of the greatest public works; some of the loftiest mountain-ranges, the vastest rivers, the healthiest and most beautifully varies seasons." His immediate contribution to images of prairie man, I suppose, is this: "Her Valley of Saskatchewan alone, it has been scientifically computed, will support eight hundred millions."[2]

If Hiebert and Lighthall illustrate one extreme approach that sees literature as a reflection of environment, Leslie Fiedler illustrates another extreme, one that sees environment as a creation of literature. In *The Return of the Vanishing American*, Fiedler remarks on a "fact, too obvious," he says, "to have been properly observed or understood, that geography in the United States is mythological":

> From the earliest times, American writers have tended to define their own country—and much of our literature has, consequently, tended to define itself—topologically, as it were, in terms of the four cardinal directions: a mythicized North, South, East, and West. Correspondingly, there have always been four kinds of American books: Northerns, Southerns, Easterns and Westerns. . . .[3]

It is worth observing that while Canadians generally are not aware of their own mythicized geography, some tentative critical analyses have been attempted: Northrop Frye's reviews in "Letters in Canada" in the *University of Toronto Quarterly*, for example, James Reaney's "The Canadian Poets' Predicament" and "The Third Eye", D.G. Jone's "The Sleeping Giant", and Milton Wilson's essay on "Klein's Drowned Poet," among others. Perhaps it is not accidental that for the most part such criticism concerns itself with problems of a *national* mythology. And perhaps, too, we should not be surprised to find that discussions of regional literature, especially prairie literature, tend to be sociological. It is my impression, admittedly based on scant knowledge, that regions get themselves defined in a variety of ways, all implying a certain determinism. Yet the interdisciplinary nature of a consultation like this one suggests that "prairie" means something different: a sort of complex conceptual framework within which various social inter-relationships can be viewed and understood. It is difficult to keep steadily in mind that "prairie" means nothing more than this, that it is a mental construct, a region of the human mind, a myth. No matter, studies of prairie literature, like E.A. McCourt's *The Canadian West in Fiction* and Egglestone's *The Frontier in Canadian Letters,* assume the priority of environment, and even Warren Tallman's "Wolf in the Snow," which pays such tribute to the "Intangible [called] self," involves those other "intangibles" which, he says, "decisively influence [the self's] efforts to come into presence,"[4] while Henry Kreisel in his very fine study "The Prairie: A State of Mind" seems quite unaware of any contradiction between his title and his remark, "All discussion of the literature produced in the Canadian west must of necessity begin with the impact of the landscape upon the mind."[5]

In this, Kreisel is very like McCourt who argues in *The Canadian West in Fiction* that three features will distinguish regional writing: one is accuracy in description; a second is poetic power in evoking the atmosphere of a particular environment and a third is a kind of psychological insight into the influence of a particular environment on the lives of those who inhabit it. "True regional literature," remarks McCourt, "is above all distinctive in that it illustrates the effect of particular, rather than general, physical, economic, and racial features upon the lives of ordinary men and women. It should and usually does do many other things besides, but if it does not illustrate the influence of a limited and peculiar environment it is not true regional literature."[6]

Perhaps we can appreciate that, if we accept McCourt's view of regional literature, at the very least we face a peculiar problem. It is the problem of literary realism. McCourt insists on the presence of a limited and peculiar environment accurately described. But what can "accuracy" possibly mean here? Certainly not what Ian Watt means when he says, "Formal realism is, of course, like the rules of evidence, only a convention," really just "a set of narrative procedures,"[7] no truer than the report of any other set of conventions. Certainly not what Austin Warren means when he says realism is a "literary-philosophical movement" essentially "like romanticism or surrealism."[8] Certainly not what Desmond McCarthy means when he says, "If Pecksniff were transported into the *Golden Bowl* he would become extinct."[9] The temptation is to believe that "accurate description" really means the imitation of certain cliches and stereotypes about landscape and environment.

If, in fact, we think for a moment about some of the wide variety of prairie novels (and I'm not going to name them), we can see at once that it is just this easy assumption about accuracy which destroys their possible value as a means of insight into prairie life and prairie images. Perhaps

47

this explains why regional literature is often thought to be quaint or peculiar, something off in an odd corner, or backwoods, or forgotten area, something that has been passed by. "The province or region . . . ," remarks Northrop Frye, "is usually a vestigial curiosity to be written up by some nostalgic tourist."[10] And E.K. Brown, who also insists that regional literature should possess accuracy both of fact and tone, decides that "in the end . . . regionalist art will fail because it stresses the superficial and the peculiar at the expense, at least, if not to the exclusion, of the fundamental and universal."[11]

The point we have reached in the argument is this: if it is meaningful to talk about images of prairie man, one should be able to find in, say, prairie literature a certain coherence or unity or identity, but the attempt to find this in some kind of realism or accuracy fails, because accuracy of fact and of tone is essentially superficial, if not indeed a contradiction in terms. In brief, if there is a distinctive regional prairie literature, it would have to be, in Fiedler's terms, mythic; and (as by now you will suspect) I am prepared to argue that we do find in our best writers, precisely such a mythicized world.

To take an example. For several years—about ten years I believe— W.O. Mitchell wrote a radio series, a highly successful series, called *Jake and the Kid*. These were half-hour broadcasts, stories of a prairie farm boy and his friend, the hired man, Jake, and their curious encounters with a group of oddly assorted characters in the town of Crocus, Saskatchewan; a prairie version, one could say, of Leacock's *Sunshine Sketches of a Little Town*.

Consider, for a moment, the kid's comments about history, prairie history, in one of Mitchell's stories called "Old MacLachlin Had a Farm."

> Most of the time at Rabbit Hill I don't do so well with history, because I get most of it from Jake, and Miss Henchbaw, that thinks she knows it all, says Jake doesn't know his history right. Whenever I write down Looie Riel was a tall, hungry-looking fellow that wore gold cuff links, chewed Black Judas tobacco, and had a rabbit's foot fob to his watch, she gives me a "D".
>
> But lately I been getting an "H", and that's because of Old Mac's coulee, that some folks call Indian Writing Place because on the rocks at the south end she's all covered over with Indian writing. . . . Ever since we started taking up where Indians roamed over the Crocus district, I been spending a lot of time around Mac's coulee. Whenever I find an arrow-head, I take her to school and get a good mark. Since I started this spring, I've found a war club, the red stone part of a peace pipe, two dozen arrow-heads, a bone-handled razor, and three dozen beer bottles.[12]

But Mac's coulee is not only history, it's geography too, a world of its own, a very special one at that. "Here's how she is," says the Kid:

Still, still as water, with the sun coming kind of streaky through the wolf willow along her edges—what you might call stiff sunlight the way she's full of dust dancing all along her. And when you lie on your belly at the bottom of Mac's coulee, you're in a world; she's your own world, and there's nobody else's there, and you can do what you want with her. You can look close at the heads on the wild oats all real feathery;
you can look at the crocuses and they're purple, not out-and-out purple, but not blue either. If you look real close they got real, small hairs like on a person's face close to a mirror. And there's tumbleweeds caught down there; they make you think about umbrellas that got their cloth ripped off them—like bones only not stary-white like a buffalo skull. Dead plants are better than anything animal that's dead.[13]

And finally Mac's Coulee is legend, the legend of the buffalo jumping pound that Jake tells the kid, the legend of how Jake saved the South Blackfoot from starvation by rounding up and trapping thousands of buffalo in the first mud blizzard to ever hit Saskatchewan.

"There wuz a million red lights a-shinin' through the dust" [says Jake, explaining how one could see the buffalo in the night of dust their stampede created,] a million red lanterns where their eyes wuz, two million bloodshot eyes that lit her up. An' the smell—she wuz enough tuh give a badger the heartburn—like the inside of a blacksmith shop a mile square with a million blacksmiths shoein' a million horses—that wuz how she smelled. They wuz runnin' on smoking hoofs—red hot, they wuz comin' so fast. An' then they hit that there cliff where the fence angled in. They wuz water there in them days. Soon as them buffalo commenced to go over, there come a hissin' an' a roarin' an' a blowin'—cloud a steam came up from them four million hoofs hittin' that there water—scalded 15 braves and 15 ponies to death. The rest got caught in the blizzard."
"Blizzard!"
"Yep. Never seen nothin' like it. Steam hit the dust, turned her to mud, an' she started in to mud. She mudded 15 feet a mud in half an hour—the first mud blizzard I ever see—50 Weasel Tail's braves got smothered to death a-sittin' on their ponies."
I looked at Jake a minute. "Jake," I said, "that's real hist'ry. That's— hist'ry."[14]

When we isolate the features of this story we find, first, a particularized landscape or locale viewed with startling clarity and in minute detail; we have a child who observes or who is seen in the landscape; we have an adult who, either in himself, or in his stories, is a grotesque—the teller of tall tales, the story-teller; we hear the particular speech of a region— dialect; and because dialect is a deviation from standard English, and standard English is thought to be literary English, we have the sense of an anti-literary form; and finally, we have humour in the ludicrous, the grotesque, the tall tale.

The features we find here, I suggest, appear in conjunction in prairie writing more frequently than we might suspect. It is particularly interesting to notice how often the child-figure is connected with the prairie landscape: in McCourt's *Walk Through the Valley,* for example; in Stegner's *Wolf Willow;* in Gabrielle Roy's *Street of Riches;* and, of course, in Mitchell's *Who Has Seen the Wind.* Other less obvious manifestations of the child I propose to come to in a few moments. Here, the point I want to make is that the regional world is essentially the world of childhood, as it is, for example, in other versions of Canadian regionalism, in James Reaney's Stratford, in Alden Nowlan's Maritimes, in Richler's Montreal (if we want to call Montreal a region), in Leacock's Mariposa, and in the most enduring of all Canadian regions, the P.E.I. of *Anne of Green Gables.*

Why the Child figure? One obvious reason is that from the adult's point of view the child's vision is a vision of innocence, of a lost Eden; another way of putting this is that the child's vision—again from the adult's point of view—is of home; and that surely is the essence of what we mean by a region, the overpowering feeling of nostalgia associated with the place we know as the *first* place, the *first* vision of things, the *first* clarity of things. Not realism, then, but rather what in painting is called magic realism, the qualities we associate with Alex Colville's paintings. Perhaps, not incidently, Ron Bloore, one of a regional school of painters, speaks of Colville as a regionalist, presumably because Colville's work evokes with extraordinary clarity objects, people, places in a design at once objective and dream-like. It is precisely the magical clarity, mistaken for accuracy, that we find in Mitchell's superb descriptions of how a boy becomes aware of objects throughout *Who Has Seen the Wind.*

The child, then, is the focus of nostalgia for the place that was—and regional literature is then a literature of a past. One of the most precise expressions of this point of view, in fact, can be found in Leacock's *Sunshine Sketches.* Where is Mariposa? The Envoi to *Sunshine Sketches* tells us: it is a region of the mind, a memory, a dream of innocence.

But if regional writing moves back in time to a magical land (as in Huck's reverie on the river with Jim) where everything is crystal clear in its most minute detail, it moves also to a world where anything can happen—where all the stories adults tell are tall tales, where our real history is myth, "a mite too rich fer Miss Henchbaw," as Jake would say, "a mite too rich fer folks that are fussy about hist'ry book hist'ry, the kind that like her sort a watered down." After all, from the child's point of view, the smallest objects appear in incredible detail and the largest, distorted, ludicrous, grotesque. Levi-Strauss, incidentally, speculates whether "the small-scale model or miniature . . . may not in fact be the universal type of the work of art." Even a larger-than-life statue may be said to be a model, he comments, since "it restores what is at first from a distance seen as a rock to the proportions of a man."[15]

The prairie as a myth of childhood? It isn't all that difficult to anticipate objections. What then do we say about the novels of Grove, Ostenso, Sinclair Ross, or about those other novels that do not touch on landscape but take as their setting the city and as their subject the crisis of immigrant life, novels like Adele Wiseman's *The Sacrifice*, John Marlyn's *Under the Ribs of Death*, and Kreisel's *The Betrayal?* I wonder whether the argument is being forced in any way if we focus on the fact that in the majority of the works I have mentioned a major feature is the conflict of generations. The myth of childhood has two forms: a comic one, in which the child is identified with the land, and a tragic one, in which the child is alienated from the land. The alienation easily takes shape as a conflict of father and son, often over the treatment of the land itself, as in Grove's novels, or as a conflict of father and daughter with incestuous implications about the nature of liberated instinct, as in Ostenso's *Wild Geese*.

Alternately, the tragic form takes shape as a father's search for a child, as in Grove's *Over Prairie Trails* and Ross's *As for Me and My House*.

Discussing the nature of the impact of prairie landscape on mind, Dr. Kreisel traces out in detail such themes as these I am now concerned with: the extraordinary sense of confinement by vast and seemingly unlimited space; the anxieties sharpened by this confinement; the definition of self by violation or conquest of land, a conquest which, he says, involves much more violence than we have been yet able to admit, even in our literature; the price paid by the conqueror; the sense of being possessed by the land; the austere puritanism bred in that harsh world; and the melodramatic eruptions of passion because of such restraint; the theme of the imprisoned spirit.[16]

This is an extraordinarily fine and perceptive list of major themes—or images, if you will—of prairie man. For Kreisel, the unifying theme is that of the impact of a particular environment. All that I could add is that I would go further and find the unifying theme and images in the mind itself, projecting *onto* the land its image of its redemptive powers in the figure of a child, and its image of demonic powers in a hostile father or tyrant who is the land.

Not the western, but the northern, says Leslie Fiedler:

> The Northern tends to be tight, gray, low-keyed, underplayed, avoiding melodrama where possible—sometimes, it would seem, at all costs. Typically, its scene is domestic, an isolated household set in a hostile environment. The landscape is mythicized New England, "stern and rockbound," the weather deep winter: a milieu appropriate to the austerities and deprivation of Puritanism.[17]

Well, the prairie "Northern" is not quite the same as the U.S. "Northern" or the Ontario Idyll or the Maritime tale, but it has a shape and a characteristic tone, and a distinguishing attitude. The distinctive element of prairie literature is not, surely, the creation of a new man, but the adaptation of images of the environment to a pattern that belongs to all men. One doesn't have to be extraordinarily perceptive, in fact, to observe how frequently the determining pattern in prairie writing is literary.

The pattern shows itself most obviously in conscious myth-makers like Adele Wiseman or Wilfred Watson (and indeed Watson's poems on Emily Carr and Calgary are brilliant examples of the kind) but it appears elsewhere too. It is in McCourt's curious blend of Conrad, Yeats, Hardy, and Wordsworth, designed to insist on the essential loneliness and loss in each human being; it informs the Wordsworthian view of childhood that Mitchell imposes on his Rousseauistic sense of the natural world; and it shows up on Ostenso's mixing of Scandinavian mythology and Freudianism. Such literary and academic overtones tell us that essentially the world being observed is a mental one. The images of prairie man are images of a search for home and therefore a search for the self.

The question we have come to then is not *who* is prairie man, but *what images* does he choose? We began by suggesting that the term "prairies" means a conceptual framework. We can conclude by suggesting that the prairie artist chooses images that help to fill in that conceptual framework. According to Levi-Strauss, the image keeps a future place open for ideas not yet present. It exists then in the realm of possibilities. Perhaps that is why the artist always moves between the end toward which he is impelled and the beginning where all was foretold. Perhaps that is why a young poet like John Newlove seeks his roots in Indian lore and wanders the highways of the province as distracted and obsessive as Grove in the Manitoba winter half a century ago.

Recently, one of our best and most distinguished writers published a book called *Documentaries*. "I like authenticity in reportage," she comments in her Forward. True enough. But I may be excused for finding in Dorothy Livesay's authentic work, the outlines of the story I have been tracing here. Her summary is all we need.

Returning to Canada after some years in Africa, Dorothy Livesay wanted to discover her country once again:

> To get the feel of my own country again I drove with my son Peter from Vancouver to my birthplace, Winnipeg. It was mid-May, with spring well started in British Columbia, but just beginning to show in the mountains and on the prairies. So we had tulips and lilacs all the way, unfolding anew in each city. By the time we reached Winnipeg I was steeped in sensations, so reminiscent of my childhood, of black soil sliding into open sky. Although I had originally hoped to write an objective documentary—a "cross-country checkup" from the Pacific to the Atlantic—I ended up abruptly and subjectively in Winnipeg. My beginnings were there. I knew: Manitoba, pivotal, facing east and west, could be the right place for an ending.[18]

NOTES

1. Paul Hiebert, *Sarah Binks* (Toronto: NCL, 1964), p. xviii.

2. W.D. Lighthall, "Introduction to Songs of the Great Dominion, 1889" in *Masks of Poetry*, ed. A.J.M. Smith (Toronto: NCL, 1962), pp. 17-18.

3. Leslie Fiedler, *The Return of the Vanishing American*, (New York: Stein and Day, 1968), p. 16.

4. Warren Tallman, "Wolf in the Snow", in *A Choice of Critics*, ed. George Woodcock (Toronto: Oxford University Press, 1966), p. 68.

5. Henry Kreisel, "The Prairie: A State of Mind", *Transactions of the Royal Society of Canada*, Vol. VI, Series 4 (June, 1968), p. 173.

6. Edward A. McCourt, *The Canadian West in Fiction* (Toronto: Ryerson, 1949), p. 55.

7. Ian Watt, "Realism and the Novel Form", in *Approaches to the Novel*, ed. Robert Scholes (San Francisco, 1961), p. 79.

8. Austen Warren, "Nature and Modes of Narrative Fiction", in *Approaches to the Novel*, p. 193.

9. Cited in Warren, "Nature and Modes of Narrative Fiction", p. 194.

10. Northrop Frye, "Canada and Its Poetry", in *The Making of Modern Poetry in Canada*, ed. Louis Dudek and Michael Gnarowski (Toronto: Ryerson, 1967), p. 89.

11. E.K. Brown, *On Canadian Poetry* (Toronto: Ryerson, 1943), p. 23.

12. W.O. Mitchell, *Jake and the Kid* (Toronto: Macmillan, 1961), p. 65.

13. *Ibid.*, p. 65.

14. *Ibid.*, pp. 68-69.

15. Claude Levi-Strauss, *The Savage Mind* (Chicago: University of Chicago Press, 1968), p. 23.

16. "The Prairie: A State of Mind", *passim*.

17. *The Return of the Vanishing American*, p. 16.

18. Dorothy Livesay, *The Documentaries* (Toronto: Ryerson, 1968), p. 50.

Romance and Realism
in
Western Canadian Fiction

I

Sometimes it appears as if literary and cultural history find their organizing principles not in causality but in synchronicity. Like a shooting star, the burning flare of coincidence lights up for a brief moment a whole intellectual landscape, an eerie incandescence before all collapses again into the prosaic darkness of unresolved events. Thus, while it is staggering to hear an American president proclaim the week of the moon-landing the greatest week since creation, it is even more dislocating to encounter a new Canadian anthology entitled *Creation*. One scarcely wants to suggest an occult connection between the first moon-landing and the appearance of the new anthology, let alone between Genesis itself and the Canadian publishing industry. But such is the temper of the times; the possibilities do arise. Norman Mailer, one suspects, would not find the possibility of moon madness among Canadians an unlikely consequence of the technology that put three men on the moon. Improbable, no doubt. But what is suspect as sociology may very well be the appropriate language of cultural criticism.

Posing as Mailer's usual madcap journalism, his *Of a Fire of the Moon*, for example, puts to us a most difficult critical puzzle, that of the relationship between a cultural symbol and its literal realization. What happens to lunacy after lunar landings? Can the frontiers of literature ever become actual places? To take another example: in a remarkable essay, Leo Marx considers the possibility that literary landscape can help us plan the future of actual landscape, even to the extent of clarifying the principles of urban and rural planning commissions—a point of view which at first glance seems little short of madness.[1] One tries, hopelessly, to imagine a city built to the imagination of Irving Layton. Of course, Marx points to the difficulties: the problem of connecting different kinds of discourse; the differences between speech controlled by image pat-

54

terns and speech controlled by pragmatic or practical ends, between metaphoric structures and logical statement.

I am not fond of distinctions between discursive and affective language. Far more satisfactory as critical guides, it seems to me, are Mailer's moon metaphors and moon men, positing as they do the great complex structures of culture and science opposed and interacting in ways we cannot yet even begin to understand. But whether we begin with Marx or Mailer, at least we remind ourselves of the difficulties in attempting to speak of something called realism or romance in the fiction of the Canadian West. *Creation* may be an unfortunate title, yet it does imply a tension between fiction and fact, symbol and actuality. Talking with Margaret Laurence, a conversation recorded in *Creation,* Robert Kroetsch remarks, "In a sense, we haven't got an identity until somebody tells our story. The fiction makes us real."[2] It is important to understand the implications of that comment, particularly as it applies to the fiction of Western Canada, because, like many of his contemporaries, Kroetsch has obviously reversed the usual order of things. Whatever we might mean by realism (itself a problem in literary terminology) with regard to one of its senses—the priority of circumstance to symbol—we often assume the primacy of historical and social event over the derived quality of portrayed existence. For a writer like Kroetsch, the life is in the symbol.

There is thus a problem. Contemporary Canadian writers turn to legends, mythology, and folklore that carry few of our supposed historical and social values or experiences. Michael Ondaatje's *The Collected Works of Billy the Kid* perhaps could be dismissed as an anachronism were it not that it belongs with Leonard Cohen's *Beautiful Losers,* Sheila Watson's *The Double Hook,* and Robert Kroetsch's *The Studhorse Man,* all of which are part of a contemporary primitivism, a world of romance that sorts oddly with our seasonally-adjusted social order. Of course, by no means all contemporary primitivism ignores Canadian material. Margaret Atwood discovers the wilderness behind the eyes of Susanna Moodie; Al Purdy seeks both the comic and tragic affinities of Indian, Eskimo, and contempoary Canadian life; John Newlove sees in Pawnee stories the identity of a land and its people. But whether in the form of a reincarnated Susanna Moodie at the University of Alberta in 1969 or the Dorsets living again in Ameliasburg, Ontario, the same question remains. Its proper dimensions seem to me best outlined in the work of Sheila Watson and Robert Kroetsch, for reasons I hope will be clear after I look briefly at the context within which their work takes its shape.

II

One of the magical words in literary criticism is "identity." I say "magical" because it is a word that enables a critic to maintain two contradictory notions: the notion of the writer's uniqueness and at the same time, of his representativeness. Mere forked writing animal, he lives imaginatively, and yet his work acquires social dimensions. He is only himself, largely ignorant of society and history, and yet there is in his writing a sort of metaphysical or ontological force that enables him to identify a people. So we have the common enough resort in our criticism to a notion of "the Canadian imagination."

Consider the difficulties. A casual use of the definite article elevates Canadian artists to the position of Canada's unacknowledged constitutional historians; at the same time, an unexamined ideology—nationalism—slips in, one hesitates to say for reasons of propaganda, but at least as a consequence of assuming that cultural and political aspects of Canadian life are identical and unitary.

The same problems exist in discussing regional writing and culture. To speak, for example, of something central to the imagination of Western Canada scarcely makes any sense in the light both of the variety of Western Canadian fiction and the virtual impossibility of deciding what it means to speak of the "West" itself. There is no single kind or genre of Western fiction in Canada: there are regional novels, rural novels, ethnic novels, pastorals, urban novels. And these, in turn, reflect a bewildering variety of concerns and themes: the encounter with the land; the impact of mechanization and urbanization on rural life; the curious rootlessness of the Prairie population; the conflict of generations and of varied cultural traditions. Any cultural history of Western Canada simply must begin with this problem of pluralism.

Of course, nothing I have said in any way denies the importance and value of critical and historical attempts to sort out and order these disparate materials and perhaps even to account for both the richness and variety of the literature, particularly the fiction of the West. Certainly, as social realists, we would find ourselves in such an attempt in sympathy with, say, Edward McCourt or Henry Kreisel, both of whom resort to the kind of environmentalism that sees the land itself as the determining feature of a portrayed existence. At the same time, the possibility remains that a peculiar achievement of the fiction of Western Canada is not social realism. To say this is at once to move out of some of the difficult and contradictory notions implied by the terms used, for it is no longer the historical and social, or even the geographical West, so much as the literary one, that concerns us. Equally, a value judgment is implied, a preference for one kind of writing over another. That is not necessarily wicked, even if it prefers its archetypes nude and asks for literary intelligence in its writers.

It is instructive here to think about the role of folklore in our literature. Early incongruities, like Sangster's attempt to populate the St. Lawrence with fairy creatures out of some watery version of Romantic or Victorian poetry, we dismiss as exceptions, despite not only the evidence of most Confederation poetry, but also of more immediate

examples such as Reaney's importing of Spenserian motifs in his ec-
logues for Stratford, Layton's panoply of gods and satyrs, or Margaret
Laurence's blending of Lear and the Old Testament. Literary nationalism consistently ignores the necessarily unfavourable balance of pay-
ments in literature. And whatever explanations we seek, whether Edward McCourt's view that domestic order in the West prevented the
development of a regional folklore, or the more usual version of the
repressive effect of frontier puritanism and materialism that E.K. Brown
advances, it seems we are to find our folklore outside of our own
boundaries and that we must discover once more that literary and
physical frontiers do not coincide. The oddly strained effect of Indian and
northern imagery in Canadian writing, as if Trinity College graduates
were to wear war paint, seems to me part of the same story.

But accepting that a large part of our folklore is imported, it remains
that we have to be clear about the nature of a folkloristic tradition. We
assume there is something we can call an American imagination that
takes the form of a frontier myth or story possessing, for Americans, a
powerful allegorical force. From Melville to Mailer, the same story has
been able to draw within its field all currents of American life. A contemporary version is the film *Little Big Man* which not only suggests by a
process of ironic inversion analogies between General Custer and General Westmoreland, the Cheyenne and the Vietnamese, but works out as
well the motifs of initiation through blood-letting and acquiring identity
through role-playing. Analogies and comparisons with Huck Finn are
virtually inescapable. And yet it is impossible to ignore the incongruities
in the film. The great American myth, as it happens, is played out in
Alberta by a Canadian Indian of the Squamish tribe and a Jewish boy
from Brooklyn. There are, after all, some limits to the willing suspension
of disbelief.

I mean to be literal-minded here, since I take it that Arthur Penn must
have been perfectly conscious of the sound of Dustin Hoffman's voice
just as he is conscious of the film techniques of alienation which he
employs so adroitly. His imagination, I suppose, could best be described
as literary. His films consist of a superb counterpointing of images from
the rich repertoire of cinematic allusion that he possesses; *Bonny and Clyde*,
for example, presents itself not as realism but as a film about American
films of the 1930's in which a gangster mythology took visible shape.
Fantasies, whether of the city outlaw and his beloved Model A or of the
Western outlaw and his beloved horse, remain fantasy, not reality. The
American frontier myth is myth.

In literature as in film there is an inward looking quality (an assimila-
tive, identifying force) that denies the disparities, perplexities, and contradictions of social life and historical development. This I take to be the
meaning of Frederick Philip Grove's remarks in his note to the fourth
edition of *A Search for America:*

> Imaginative literature is not primarily concerned with facts; it is con-
> cerned with truth. . . . In its highest flights, imaginative literature,
> which is one and indivisible, places within a single fact the history of
> the universe from its inception as well as the history of its future to the
> moment of its final extinction.[3]

Now that may be bad history and worse sociology, but it is first-rate criticism. It suggests that the writer's own sense of creativity and inventiveness (making it new) pulls him away from what Grove calls "fact" toward something else. That "something else" is often taken to be the realm of the subjective, the writer's dreams or feelings or imaginings or what not. But Grove indicates his meaning: paradoxically a rewriting of the traditional story. For a writer like Grove, then, the imaginative process is not a mirroring of experience, still less a dream process. It is, in the act of writing, the creation of a self or an identity. In less grandiose terms, we might want to say "an interpretation of experience," though that scarcely carries the burden of meaning Grove puts upon a word like "truth." His West is not so much discovered as created.

The point is worth pursuing a little further both because of Grove's importance as a writer of Western Canadian novels and because in the paradoxes of his life and work he so brilliantly poses the paradoxes criticism itself must face. He concerned himself with truth, yet if we are to believe Douglas Spettigue, whose study of Grove is one of the few genuinely startling pieces of detective work in Canadian scholarship, Grove altered times and details in his story. This may be so. What is equally apparent is that the outline of the story is fantasy rather than manipulated fact. But why would Grove indulge himself—if that is the appropriate term—in so *profound* a fiction, even were there facts to be concealed? Somewhere Morley Callaghan remarks that Grove was capable of believing the strangest dreams. Believing the strangest dreams, in search of himself, one could say Grove's life was created by his own fiction, his novels that—it seems now—literally wrote him into existence. "The fiction makes us real," says the younger novelist, Robert Kroetsch. And so it is. The writer's task becomes an increasingly sensitive articulation of his literary tradition—not to write up the experience of the country but to articulate the forms of its fiction. So Western Canadian fiction may be seen to involve a double process, and, to judge from comments like Grove's and Kroetsch's, one that is conscious as well: on the one hand, it involves finding forms appropriate to new sets of experience or, more exactly, the placing of new experience in its metaphorical context; on the other, it involves integrating or unifying literary experience itself, finding out, in other words, whether existing literary tradition, in all its richness and variety, connects with the "literary" materials at hand—folklore, legend, tall tale, whatever has filtered down in its curious ways from older lore which is itself part of the tradition that now seeks to connect with it.

From this point of view, more interesting than Grove's sociology of Prairie life is his use of the pastoral contrast of city and country. Similarly, it is not the highly praised depiction of Prairie boyhood that is important in W.O. Mitchell's *Who Has Seen the Wind* so much as the Wordsworthian pastoral of innocence and experience. It becomes more interesting to locate and define motifs of Scandinavian saga and figures of romance in Martha Ostenso's novels than to praise her boldness and so-called realism for daring to write surely one of the more modest nude scenes in twentieth-century literature. Farm machinery in Robert Stead's *Grain* undoubtedly depicts farm machinery, the fact of mechanization in a rural world, but just as surely images of machines are structural principles in storytelling, the purest form of which we find, in Canadian writing at least, in Archibald Lampman's "City of the End of Things." Nor is it, then, surprising that as we turn from writers of the generation of Grove, Ostenso, and Stead, to our more immediate contemporaries— Margaret Laurence, Adele Wiseman, Henry Kreisel, John Marlyn—we discover that symbolic patterning becomes more explicit, as in Henry Kreisel's use of wasteland imagery in *The Betrayal*, Margaret Laurence's use of the biblical story of Hagar in *The Stone Angel*, Adele Wiseman's retelling of the tale of Abraham and Isaac in *The Sacrifice*.

To argue that Western Canadian fiction develops an increasing awareness of its own forms ought to come as no surprise. This, after all, is the sort of argument given currency in Northrop Frye's influential criticism, and it has served in the essays of Warren Tallman and James Reaney and in Douglas Jones' *Butterfly on Rock* as the groundwork for a thematic and cultural history of Canada. An essay on the West in fiction should in fact read simply as an elaborate footnote to such criticism. But at the risk of repetition, it is worth noticing the extent to which our cultural historians, like many of our social philosophers, remain environmentalists. Our understanding of ourselves and our country would be more than impoverished were it not for the deeply felt and serious essays of George Grant and it is no matter for easy dismissal that he sees, particularly in *Technology and Empire*, the land writing itself into the Canadian imagination as surely as W.L. Morton sees the north imprinting itself on us in his own account of our character, *The Canadian Identity*. The sense that there is in this environmentalism a Protestant eschatology, to which Saint Sammy's Jeremiads might serve as appropriate choral accompaniment, does not diminish the force of the argument. Of course, regional literature, say Western Canadian fiction, is especially susceptible to an environmental approach, possibly because we tend to equate regions with particular space. But the land tells us little about genuine folkloristic elements; the western as outlaw story, the rogue figure of tall tales, ballads telling of domestic and border violence and terror. And it leaves unanswered the most peculiar question of all: in what sense could we say a fiction, particularly a fiction of America or Greece or Judea, makes us real, defines our identity?

I don't know whether questions of that sort can be answered but the reasons for asking them become apparent the moment one looks at novels like Sheila Watson's *The Double Hook* and Robert Kroetsch's *The Studhorse Man*. The former gives us the western story as parody; the latter turns the form of tall tale, odyssey, and rogue's story into metaphors of book and dream. Both, it seems to me, seek to locate Western Canadian fiction within a coherent, developing tradition and therefore to expand rather than contract its dimensions and possibilities, and though both are relatively brief, it is not reasonable to see them as encyclopaedic in range.

III

Concise and intense, *The Double Hook* relies on more than flashing phrase and oracular remark for its effects. Elaborately structured and closely integrated, like some highly-charged atomic accelerator, it radiates microcosmic suggestions of fundamental energies. So lapidary a form, of course, raises questions about the place of artifice, contrivance, and self-consciousness in literature. Yet literacy could scarcely be said to disqualify a writer, though since it appears to be a matter of degree, it might very well determine style and form. Certainly, those works which we might want to describe as "artificial" now appear not as sports but as definitions in Canadian writing. *The Double Hook* belongs with, say, the poems of James Reaney, Jay Macpherson's *The Boatman,* A.M. Klein's *The Second Scroll* (and just possibly one should add Atwood's *Journals of Susanna Moodie*), writing distinguished by its capacity to assimilate varied materials, to comment on and construct—or at least rewrite—a literary tradition. Obviously, to isolate any element of a work so carefully wrought is to do violence to it, but at the risk of distortion, it seems necessary, in the context of this discussion, to look at the element of parody in the novel.

In a perceptive introduction to the New Canadian Library edition, John Grube comments on Mrs. Watson's use of parody: her parody of folk wisdom, of the "quaintness" (as he puts it) of the ethnic novel, of the "illusions" of regionalism and of the setting and action of the western or cowboy story. In each instance, Grube tells us, the novelist attempts through parody to break out of imposed limitations—limitations of regionalism, ethnicity, and popular art—in order to arrive at a universal form. No doubt Mrs. Watson does intend to explode the limitations of provincialism and parochialism. A rough and wicked humour, not unlike that in a mediaeval morality play, cuts deliberately across the high poetic lines, the buzzing energy of the novel. I pause only to notice how the laments of a wailing widow punctuate the revelatory moments of the story: dear god, why must there be so much violence; dear god, the bacon's not done; dear god, another child in this world. The earthy incongruities offer their own comment on both homely tale and high wisdom. Thus, at the concluding nativity scene, a vision of the child like something out of Breughel:

> Dear God, said the Widow, it's a feeble cry. Quick, Quick, she called and clambered down from the box as Ara pulled the horses to a stop before the door.
>
> We don't want any trouble, Angel said as she jumped down from the seat.
>
> The Window's hand was on the knob.
>
> If there's trouble, Mrs. Prosper, she said, it won't be of my making. Dear God, she said, the latch needs oil.[4]

Yet it seems to me inadequate to view parody simply as a reductive force. Parody indeed "explodes" a form, but it may also elevate (a famous example is Pope's *Rape of the Lock*); it may be used to isolate formal elements, and, if it is so used, enable an author to work out sharply and clearly the design of the work.

Through the exaggerations and distortions of parody, then, Mrs. Watson writes an ethnic, regional western, deliberately exploiting the conventionality of the forms she has chosen to work with. The resulting work is angular, diagrammatic (though not in any way rough-hewn), for it establishes what otherwise remain obscure, possible connections between convential forms. Those connections, I believe, are its heart, the source of its incredible energy.

From the form of the ethnic novel, Mrs. Watson takes the sense of folk wisdom, as in gnomic sayings and earth-philosophizing, and the sense of community essential to her sacramental theme of sacrifice, communion, redemption. (It is not entirely an aside to note that this ethnic pattern has its Yiddish and Judaic parallel in Adele Wiseman's *The Sacrifice* and in a grotesquely inverted parody of a parody, Mordecai Richler's *Cocksure*.) From regional novels, Mrs. Watson takes the sense of place as mythic home, and for her plot line, one event, the killing of the mother. As in, say, Martha Ostenso's *Wild Geese,* or in Grove's Prairie novels and especially in *Our Daily Bread,* the suffocating closeness of family, and the murderous oppression it involves, define one extreme of regionalism, so an idyllic childhood world precariously close to the threat of adulthood— as in W.O. Mitchell's or E.A. McCourt's novels—defines the other extreme. Thematically, regionalism tends to define identity as place and community, both located within an individual and yet outside in the communal culture. If character is defined as both peculiar and representative, then we see how it is that in regional writing characterization tends toward grotesque types and caricature.

But of the three forms that provide structural principles for Mrs.

61

Watson's novel, the western is at once more compelling and puzzling than the other two. It is clear, of course, that, as the most familiar of the three, the western allows for the most extensive play; additionally, recalling films, it both opens up technical possibilities and connects immediate visual imagery with older romance forms, a point to which I shall return. One could, I suppose, object that the cowboy story sorts badly with Western Canadian history, if not our setting. Bankers and clergy rode our plains, and the Mounted Policeman, never quite large enough for myth, played the role that elsewhere was the outlaw's. My own knowledge of Canadian westerns is limited to some early writing of Edward McCourt and to Wallace Stegner's *Wolf Willow,* although, of course, only part of Stegner's work devotes itself to western material proper, a section on the Fort McLeod incident, and one on the legendary winter of 1906 and a cattle-herding story. Leslie Fiedler argues that there are not only westerns, but southerns, easterns, and northerns as well; it begins to appear that, whenever Canadian novels are neither idyllic nor pastoral, they should be something like Fiedler's version of a northern. And no less an historian than W.L. Morton argues that the contrast of pastoral and northern is a principle of Canadian life, though he seems to take this clear literary principle as a fact of geography and national character. Yet the point is not that Mrs. Watson is bound by any interpretations of this precarious society and its past. If history calls for a northern mode, apparently something else insists on a western. For Mrs. Watson, one suspects, that "something else" is literary design: desert setting, dry land, stereotyped characters, community, town, outsider, the pattern of a good-bad, black-white contrast, all connected with notions of law and outlaw, justice and revenge, murder and hanging. It should be apparent now that with the design of the western, the formal pattern of her novel is complete: home and community become as elemental as place itself, while out of elemental design is born the terrifying poem that is at one and the same time the voice of a god and the voice of an animal howling in the night:

> I have set his feet on soft ground
> I have set his feet on the sloping shoulders
> of the world. (p. 134)

The western tale unifies the novel because it enables Mrs. Watson to take the forms in which our imagination expresses itself—regional novel, ethnic story, the cycle of generation—and show us the connections between them and a larger imaginative world that extends to Shakespeare and the Bible. The forms with which we perceive ourselves in our own society (or the metaphorical form of our society) then may be seen as part of a larger pattern that is the pattern of Western culture itself, at least its romance pattern of questing knight and mysterious grail. That story, we have been told more than once, links together images of a stranger riding out of desert country, a people in bondage in Egypt, a wandering in the wilderness, a return to a promised land; it connects images of dry land and water with the mysteries of aloneness, community, justice, and mercy.

It is, surely, difficult to contemplate the fierce images of *The Double Hook*—the old lady fishing, the blazing furnace of valley and house, messengers in the dry land—without recalling something of the iconography of *The Wasteland, The Tempest,* and the Bible. But it isn't difficult to anticipate objections: that either this interpretation of the novel is mechanical or the novel itself is a machine; that where literature presents itself as myth rather than experience, its contrivance fails to create that authentic human world we ask of even our most learned writers. One answer, of course, is that *The Double Hook* need fear nothing from the limitations of this commentator. It would be unforgiveable to identify the work with an interpretation in order to dismiss it. By the same token, it would be a misrepresentation of the novel to ignore its deliberately diagrammatic quality. More important than one's taste in matters of iconography is an understanding that allusiveness—the use of convention and parallel story in what T.S. Eliot, commenting on Joyce's *Ulysses,* called the mythic method—seeks those metaphors that put local story and fable into the context of the literature of a whole culture. To speak of the result as artifice is not a value judgment so much as a description.

Still, a more accessible version of the mythic method is that in which myth presents itself as experience, not literature. In lurid tales of rogue and fool, for example, we feel we can discern a recognizable world, for no matter how oddly tilted it might be, it is after all distorted only to the extent that the hero of the tall tale proves to be himself eccentric, one of the town's oddities: the Old Ben, beer-parlour raconteur extraordinary; Saint Sammy, wild man of the Prairies, counting underwear labels in his piano-box house; Jake, the hired man, whose sense of history is defined purely by his mastery of contradiction; all are rogue-fool figures, part of a tradition in Canadian writing that goes back at least to Sam Slick, Yankee pedlar and ring-tailed roarer, and includes such varied fool-innocents as Earle Birney's Turvey, Mordecai Richler's Duddy Kravitz, and as the latest honourable addition, Hazard Lepage, or perhaps more accurately, the narrator of Lepage's story in Robert Kroetsch's *The Studhorse Man.*

Like his forebears, Lepage is a questing knight, a displaced Ulysses seeking not only his Penelope but a mare for his great stallion, Poseidon. Yet to present the story as myth does not do it justice. For experience, an intensely realized world, plays an extraordinary part in this novel, and it is the role of experience that I want to look at. Certainly the story is grounded in place: coulee, gulch, boneyard, Edmonton's 109th street and its Woodwards, river, bridge, farmyard, and schoolhouse, all presented with that particularity and lucidity characteristic of more than one

Prairie novel, Mitchell's *Who Has Seen the Wind*, for example. And even the wild wandering events, grotesque and off-centre as if viewed through a flawed glass, seem at least possible, if not probable: a Ukrainian wedding remembered as through a glass dimly; a Doukhobour-like school-burning; a night in a museum; a beer-parlour horse-trading session; a brawl in a boneyard; a discovery of a use for mare's urine. Familiar, yet so distorted in the novel that one looks again at the familiar, doubting its validity. For, remarkably, this Alberta and all its people, including it seems the reader, turn into a book and a dream. To suggest the energy— ferocious, bawdy, hilarious—involved in that transformation could very well exceed any normal critical capacity and certainly the decorum of this article. But Kroetsch's method, at least, can be indicated.

On the one hand, experience turns into a book, rather as everything turns into clothes in *Sartor Resartus*. Almost compulsively the narrator insists on turning events into lists, genealogies, catalogues, histories, and more often than not for him the lists gravitate, as his world does, toward a subsuming metaphoric vision, the radical metaphor implied in the title of the book, man as stud horse. Horse, itself, as we shall see, is as much art as life. On the other hand, as we begin to comprehend the complex narrative structure and understand who tells the story and from what vantage point, experience dissolves into dream.

Book metaphors appear even in the hero's name, Lepage, at once "the page written upon" and a glue label. The label-man, now labelled, is also horse-man (studhorse man), fabulous creature out of a mythic past. More pervasively, the book metaphor makes itself felt as we encounter catalogues and genealogies: genealogies of horses; genealogies of men. It is as if generation itself, that *axis mundi* on which, as the narrator redundantly remarks, wise men tell us the world itself turns, had been transformed into a catalogue. To take one example: *The General Stud Book* rests on the bookshelves beside Hazard's desk in the great house where he lives with his horses and his seven beds. The desk and its contents are presented to us with the sharpness and presence of experienced life. So we hear of

> currycombs, a broken hamestrap, a spoon wired to a stick for dropping poisoned wheat into the holes of offending gophers, saltpetre, gentian root, a scattering of copper rivets, black antimony, a schoolboy's ruler, three mousetraps in a matchbox, two chisels for trimming hoofs, Cornucrescine (for making horn grow), ginger, horse liniment and liniment for his back, Elliman's Royal Embrocation, blue vitriol, an electuary, nux vomica, saddle soap in a Spode (a simple blue and white) saucer. Spanish fly. . . .[5]

A list surely worthy of that famous one Huck gives us as he catalogues his findings in the house of the dead, this one is immediately followed by the genealogy of horses from the book of studs that, we are told, is Hazard's poetry and philosophy, his history of man and his theology.

And as we read with Hazard of the horse world, we can wonder which is real, the desk or the book, and whether one dissolves into the other:

> The old book opened of itself to the list of brood mares, and Hazard read defiantly the words he could so easily quote: ALCIDES MARE, *Bred by Mr. Bland, in 1764, her dam by Crab, out of Snap's dam.* Hazard, let me explain, was no loafing, snivelling schoolmarm of a man: those words were pain to him. Those beautiful words. He read on: BLANK MARE, *Foaled in 1755, her dam, Dizzy, by Driver.* . . . Don't you see why he read, why he ached, why he had to read? Let me go on, for I, too, on lonely afternoons, have sought out that dark volume: *Dizzy, by Driver—Smiling Tom—Miss Hipp, by Oysterfoot—Merlin—Commoner—D. of Somerset's Coppin Mare.* Not that Hazard wept as I have. Hazard cursed. 'God damn the damned,' he said. . . . He must have put a stained finger to the old print. He cursed and read on, caught in and dreading that beautiful dead mad century: A-LA-GREQUE . . . *got by Regulus—her damn by Allworthy—grandam by Bolton Starling—great grandam, Dairy Maid, by Bloody Buttocks.* . . . (pp. 10-11)

The ceremony of naming continues with other catalogues: of the Lepage family, of the Proudfoots (Martha, Thatcher, Toreador, Tennyson, and Titmarsh Proudfoot), of the hockey players of Canada, the food and drink at a Ukrainian wedding, the diseases of the horse. It is as if the novel itself, certainly the narrator of the novel, is driven by the desperate need to classify everything, as in a book, and to see it all arranged finally as a taxonomy of the horse, for its cry is, in the narrator's own words, "The exquisitely piercing mortal cry, the cry half horse, half man, the horse-man cry of pain or delight or eternal celebration at what is and what must be." (p. 163)

But if the moving principle of the novel is the horse—Poseidon, giver of life, *mer*, mare, mother, father—the horse of Kroetsch's fictional world must be described in images not of Prairie life but of Chinese art:

> It strikes me that I have been remiss in describing, not this perverse human caricature of the essential animal, but that animal itself. Let me make amends, my dear reader; and I can best describe Poseidon by referring you to the superlative grace and beauty of Chinese art.
>
> I hardly know where to suggest you begin. Those old Chinese artists: they drew their horses true to life, true to the rhythm of life. They dreamed their horses and made the horse too. They had their living dream of horses. . . . Ah, where to begin? Why is the truth never where it should be? Is the truth of the man in the man or in his biography? Is the truth of the beast in the flesh and confusion or in the few skilfully arranged lines. . . . But study for one day that one horse—Han Kang's bold creation, Shining Light of the Night. . . . Our pitiful world: we pack a corpse off in copper and steel that it might for an extra year bewilder the dust. And yet one horse for the spirit's night and we would be immortal. . . . (pp. 130-131)

But if the horse (and horse-man) can best be realized in images of art and book that resolve "the flesh and confusion" in a "few skilfully arranged lines," both art and book themselves dissolve into dream. The one who tells this story of horses, we discover, sits naked in a bathtub in a mental institution, viewing the world through a clever arrangement of mirrors that enables him to see where the action of the novel once took place, though its past is now his present. Possessed by Hazard's dream, as Hazard was possessed by Poseidon, the narrator looks at mirror images of mirror images. What follows though is worse, the suggestion that the dream includes ourselves: ". . . we are all, so to speak, one . . . each of us is, possibly, everyone else. . . ." (p. 115)

We have been dreamed by our fiction. A preposterous claim, surely. Those clumsy tales. Those distortions. The exaggeration. The falsification of history. How little to the point about the labour movement of the thirties, about Jewish immigrant families in Hirsch or Hoffer, Saskatchewan, about narrow cities in their pride and greed and oil. Only, say, Sinclair Ross's *As For Me and My House* to tell of how (in Grove's phrase) the wilderness uses up human material. Only Robert Stead's *Grain*, a creaking vehicle for the realities of farm life. We expected the land itself would speak, as Grove dreamed it might, but it has not been so. Not the land, but art. Not experience, but vision.

It is perhaps too easy to put the differences between Watson's work and Kroetsch's as the differences between myth as literature and myth as experience. It is equally easy to say one is a closed structure that simply diagrams a literary pattern and the other an open structure that seeks to turn experience itself into representative pattern. These distinctions may serve critical or literary purposes of evaluation but say little to the point about the nature of dream romance, and identity. My own sense is that the literature of Western Canada has its own coherence, not in relation to place, society, or history, but to its own developing forms. And with Kroetsch's novel, the fiction of the West looks back not only to the forms from which it grew but to the literature that it has brought into existence. Paradoxically, a Western Canadian myth becomes possible in the contemporary world as the writer assimilates the techniques, patterns, and vision of Faulkner, Barth, Borges, and Nabokov, and presents to us as our own identity a fiction dreamed by writers of America, Europe, and South America. Nor is that all: the fiction that dreams us proves in the end to have been a madman's dream. For the horse lives on with the discovery of a use for pregnant mare's urine, a dream of art become technology. Now, and I use the narrator's words, "Scurrilous, barbarous, stinking man would soon be able, in the sterility of his own lust, to screw himself into oblivion." (p. 167) The future of Western Canada seems even more tenuous than a passing dream.

IV

I doubt it possible to improve on the theme, as a conclusion to this paper, of the disappearing West. And these last remarks simply elaborate that. I began by suggesting how little could be said about difficult critical questions and how little we know about cultural history. It should be clear now that nothing said in this paper in any way relieves our ignorance. Claims to the contrary notwithstanding, it seems to me eminently sensible to remain sceptical about what has been added to our knowledge of the Canadian West by discussions or literary depictions of regional cultures. Like cultural nationalism, the fictional West contributes little, if anything, to discussion in this country of educational policy, constitutional arrangements, or political theory, and it proves nothing at all about the quality of provincial government or even Prairie life.

To say, then, as Robert Kroetsch says, that we have no identity until someone tells our story, that fiction makes us real, is not paradoxical but tautological. The statement surely means identity is fictional; it exists only in stories, in dreams, in fantasy. About this, we may say one of two things: fantasy plays no historical or social role *or* its role is much stranger than anything we yet know. There are those—writers like George Steiner, Susan Sontag, George Grant—who remind us from a variety of perspectives and convictions that there are questions to be asked of the spiritual enterprise that is Western culture.

Not to be implicated in history, of course, implies an incredible intellectual hubris. But to claim historical and social validity for the worlds of fiction may have even wider and more disturbing implications. What are the consequences of claiming a defining presence where there is none, an identity where (to use the term as George Grant uses it) there is only technique? And why, after all, should a wind-blown, dust-driven, rootless place, its people eager for the limitless power of productivity, be proclaimed that world, favoured among all others, where a long lost—if ever held—wholeness finally reveals itself?

NOTES

1. Leo Marx, "Pastoral Ideals and City Troubles", *The Quality of Man's Environment* (Washington, D.C., 1968), pp. 121-144.

2. *Creation,* ed. Robert Kroetsch (Toronto: New Press, 1970), p. 63.

3. Frederick Philip Grove, "Author's Note to the Fourth Edition", *A Search for America* (Toronto: NCL, 1971).

4. Sheila Watson, *The Double Hook* (Toronto: McClelland and Stewart, 1966), p. 130. All other references are to this edition.

5. Robert Kroetsch, *The Studhorse Man* (Toronto: Macmillan, 1969), p. 10. All other references are to this edition.

Writing West:
On the Road
to Wood Mountain[1]

The subject of regionalism in Canadian writing has come in for more discussion lately than one would expect in a predominantly nationalist atmosphere but it is probably worth going over the ground once again, if only to see where the confusions may be, or simply to provide a personal perspective. The theoretical basis of literary regionalism is rather less firm than the historical or geographical but a sense persists that writers work out of locale or area, boundaries of some sort defining sensibility. Whether it follows that personal experience can contribute to the discussion remains problematical but writers generally do insist on either the uniqueness of experience or at least the importance of an individual point of view and inevitably any talk of place gets mixed up with one's own sense of particularity. At any rate, it seems to me important to try to say something about my sense of where I stand in relation to place in poetry; maybe once and for all to find out in the very process of writing where and how the west, the prairies, Estevan, fit into a personal mythology, into the sounds and rhythms of a voice, images, definitions. And, of course, even to attempt to say this is to recognize one is not alone but part of a pattern, part of a cultural development. There could be no other reasons for making the attempt.

Some years ago Milton Wilson suggested that the real virtues of Canadian writing might very well lie in our often criticized colonialism and regionalism. Our perspectives, he suggested, have something to do with boundaries and contrasting patterns; not with place so much as with motion:

> The nomadic culture of contemporary N/A makes the wandering poet the norm, and in as varied a country as Canada he is always having to set his digestion on fresh images—from 'Dawn on Anglo-Saxon Street' to 'Dusk on English Bay', from the ambiguous Avon flowing through Stratford, Ontario, to an equally ambiguous streetcar running down Main Street in Winnipeg, from the 'blue men of Saskatchewan' to the

'blue women of Quebec' and more than back again, from Newfound-
land to the Last Spike. Indeed, the poet who moves west (or returns
west) already has a niche in our gallery of poet archetypes right
opposite the poet who can never get out of Montreal.

I must admit that before recalling Wilson's remarks I was a bit uneasy
about presenting myself as a *Western writer.* Ten years in Toronto, it
seemed to me, hardly qualifies one as a poet of the prairies. But if Wilson
can be taken seriously, it is not place alone that matters but a direction,
an attraction—something like the movement of a compass needle; not
where it is, but where it points matters. My image for the prairie writer
then, at least as a point of beginning for this account, is not necessarily
the one who is in the west, or who stays here, but the one who returns,
who moves, who points in this direction.

I know this too can sound heretical or like special pleading but it fits
very closely my own sense that it is not place but attitude, state of mind,
that defines the western writer—and that state of mind, I want to
suggest has a good deal to do with a tension between place and culture, a
doubleness or duplicity, that makes the writer a man not so much in
place, as out of place and so one endlessly trying to get back, to find his
way home, to return, to write himself into existence, writing west.

A lot of regional criticism, I know, concentrates on place: Laurence
Ricou in *Vertical Man/Horizontal World,* Edward McCourt in that fine and
important and early work *The Canadian West in Fiction,* Henry Kreisel
(despite the title of his article: "The Prairies: A State of Mind"), George
Woodcock, who in a recent article on Canadian poetry in the *London Times
Literary Supplement* concludes by noting how important place and land have
become in Canadian and especially western Canadian writing, referring
particularly to Suknaski, Marty, Newlove. Place and Land. I remember
how moved I was when last year I first heard Andrew Suknaski read at
Banff from his *Wood Mountain Poems* and how I thought: that's the book I
should have written, its terrible authenticity, its powerful directness, its
voices and places echoing in its time and truth. This is a book I'll come
back to later. Just now, I note that Suknaski puts the point I want to make
in his own comments about his work: "For me *Wood Mountain Poems* is a
return to ancestral roots in my birth place, after seventeen years of
transience and aberration in numerous Canadian cities—and of trying to
find the meaning of home." He then turns to that doubleness I mentioned
a moment ago, that divided sense in this writer that makes his vision not
only complex but fascinating: "The poems also deal with a vaguely
divided guilt; guilt for what happened to the Indian (his land taken)
imprisoned on his reserve; and guilt because to feel this guilt is a betrayal
of what you ethnically are—the son of a homesteader and his wife who
must be rightfully honoured in one's mythology." Suknaski's "well-
remembered story" then is built of all those complicated motifs; aberration, guilt, division, betrayal—not, in other words, folksiness, nostal-

69

gia, description, or even realism but "one's own mythology."

It occurs to me how many writers 'writing west' are those who leave and return: Robert Kroetsch, for example, from New York State to the badlands of Alberta; John Newlove, from the badlands of McClelland and Stewart's office in Don Mills, Ontario, to the plains of Saskatchewan—at least in memory and desire; W.O. Mitchell, Adele Wiseman, Dorothy Livesay, Margaret Laurence—the list can go on, despite, of course, those who stay and write, or move and return in a totally different sense. So it isn't place that we have to talk about but something more complicated and more compelling: remembered place—or beyond that—remembered self, something lost and recovered, a kind of memory, a kind of myth.

Writing about another novelist who returns west, Ann Mandel sees Wallace Stegner's "neglected history" *Wolf Willow* as a work about a place that exists in a kind of frontier, not *in* Stegner's personal history or *in* the 'actual' history of the area, but "more accurately . . . *between* them, for it is the frontier between memory and history that attracts Stegner." "The frontier," she says, "runs through his imagination between the search for the self and the writing of a book. The 'ancient unbearable' moment of recognition belongs on one side, Stegner's mental geography on the other, and the link is literature: style." She quotes Stegner: "there is a kind of provincialism . . . that encompasses the most profound things a writer has to say."

I turn to Stegner's book, and Ann's article on it here, partly because Ann is writing out of our own experience of returning to Eastend-Whitemud—Stegner's town; returning, I say, though we had never been there before, except in the book; partly because Stegner's own return to his childhood home sets up the kind of doubleness that is my own concern; partly because the book brings me closest to the kind of personal experience that I want to record in this paper—the muse of Estevan itself. For of all the things that Stegner's book is—and that includes a history, a memoir, a legend—a story and memory of the last plains frontier, as he puts it, an extraordinary account of a man and a writer recalling how it was to grow up, to be a boy in a small town on the prairies—of all this, it is most significantly an account (I use Ann's words here) of "the function of culture in a society and . . . his own role as a writer, a book in search of himself and his own identity." And for our purposes, there is among many passages, one that strikes most truly home:

> . . . every frontier child knows exactly who he is, and who his mother is, and he loves his alarm clock quite as much as if it had feathers. But then comes something else, a waddling thing with webbed feet, insisting that *it* is his mother, that he is not who he thought he was, but infinitely more, heir to swans and phoenixes. In such a town as White-mud, school superimposes five thousand years of Mediterranean culture and two thousand years of Europe upon the adapted or redis-covered simplicities of a new continent. . . . If there is truth in Law-

rence's assertion that America's unconscious wish has always been to destroy Europe, it is also true that from Irving to William Styron, American writers [I would add, Canadian too] have been tempted to apostasy and expatriation, toward return and fusion with the parent. It is a painful and sometimes fatal division, and the farther you are from Europe—that is, the farther you are out in the hinterlands of America—the more difficult it is. Contradictory voices tell you who you are. You grow up speaking one dialect and reading and writing another. During twenty-odd years of education and another thirty of literary practice you may learn to be nimble in the King's English; yet in moments of relaxation, crisis, or surprise you fall back into the corrupted lingo that is your native tongue. Nevertheless all forces of culture and snobbery are against you writing by ear and making contact with your natural audience. . . . You grow out of touch with your dialect because learning and literature lead you another way unless you consciously resist. It is only the occasional Mark Twain or Robert Frost who manages to get the authentic American tone of voice into his work. For most of us, the language of literature is to some extent unreal, because school has always been separate from life.

It has been said before, of course. And in Canadian terms too. The gap between culture and nature, the European-American tension, these have been talked about from different, even opposite points of view by writers like E.K. Brown, Northrop Frye, Warren Tallman, and a host of others, but for my purpose, Stegner's version of it, like Robert Kroetsch's later account, is the important one because it strikes so close to home, because he writes about the place and language and experience I know, articulating the west of my own experience.

The return from Toronto to Estevan is a long one, by way of Eastend, to Cypress Hills and Wood Mountain, and through time back some forty years. It is Sept. 1931. At the rim of the Souris Valley, a ramshackle green clapboard house rattles and creaks in the unceasing wind, the "pushing and shouldering wind" Stegner calls it, in those years always gritty with dust, the topsoil lifting, blowing away. My father is in Meadow Lake, or some other god-forsaken town, trying to sell, of all incredible things, Fuller Brushes. We have no money. The house groans. My mother is reading poetry to me—poetry!—from *Elbert Hubbard's Scrap Book:*

> When Earth's last picture is painted
> and the tubes are twisted and dried,
> When the oldest colors have faded, and
> the youngest critic has died,
> We shall rest, and, faith, we shall need
> it—lie down for an eon or two,
> Till the Master of All Good Workmen
> shall set us to work anew!
>
> And those that were good shall be happy:
> they shall sit in a golden chair;
> They shall splash at a ten-league canvas
> with brushes of comet's hair;
> They shall find real saints to draw from—

Magdalene, Peter, and Paul;
They shall work for an age at a sitting
and never be tired at all![2]

"L'Envoi," by Rudyard Kipling

It's enough, as W.O. Mitchell puts it, to give a gopher the heartburn. You have to know Elbert Hubbard's work to appreciate the extraordinary irony, the collosal disparity in the situation: the gap between literature and life. The *Scrap Book*, we're told in the subtitle, contains "the inspired and inspiring selections gathered during a life time of discriminating reading for his own use." The coalminers of Bienfait were gathering to march on the town of Estevan. Steel-helmeted RCMP posted machine guns at what they called strategic corners and streets. Jewish farmers like my grandfather abandoned the hopeless dry dying farms. And the publishers of Elbert Hubbard—that is to say Hubbard himself—tell us "He was merely gathering spiritual provisions for his own refreshment and dedication. To glance at the pages of his *Scrap Book* is to realize how far and wide he pursued the Quest, into what scented rose gardens of Poetry, and up what steep slopes of Thought To Alpine Valleys of classical literatures it led him, and through forests and swamps of contemporary writing." Beautifully produced, with its illuminated red capital letters, its bold faced type, the book collects gems and flowers from a most astonishing variety of sources: say, to take a list at random, Dickens, John Quincy Adams, Israel Zangwill, George Horace Lorimer, Goethe, Robert Louis Stevenson, Theodore Roosevelt, G. Lowes Dickinson, Samuel Johnson, Cavour, Franklin, Joseph Conrad, Grenville Kleiser, William Wister. And it treats us to such aphoristic wisdom as J.C. Holland's: "Music was a thing of the soul—a rose lipped shell that murmured of the eternal sea—a strange bird singing the songs of another shore." Outside the green clapboard house, another Russian thistle bounded by. "Life is but a Thought" remarks Coleridge. Somebody carves *murdered by the RCMP* on the gravestone of a dead miner. "The nation that has schools has the future," remarks Bismarck.

There's more, of course. All those bad poems that somehow stuck in my mind and became the forms and language I would always have to work with: Henley's "Invictus"; Fisher's "I met her on the Umbrian Hills"; Bourdillon's "The night has a thousand eyes"; Dana Miller's "And This I Hate"; and the writers: Stevenson, Vachel Lindsay; Rupert Brooke; Alfred Noyes; Christina Rossetti; Alice Meynell; Tennyson; Bliss Carman; the whole panoply of 19th century versification ranging as it does from the impossibly sublime to the intense inane. But the point surely is that the irony to which I'm drawing attention now entirely escaped me then. In that poor shabby house surrounded by the devastated land and indeed in very peril of our lives, the high-minded sentimentality of those words moved across my mind like a vision of real human possibility. Never mind that, like Stegner, I wasn't even aware that "the information

I was gaining from literature and from books on geography and history had not the slightest relevance to the geography, history, or life of the place where I lived" or that living in Estevan I didn't even know I lived there. The life of the mind and the life of the body had been radically separated, compartmentalized. Mentally, I was being brought up as a genteel Victorian boy, with a quaint though serious touch of middle-European Yiddish gentility to boot. Physically, emotionally, like Stegner and in his words, I was a sensuous little savage. The contradictions didn't strike me then; only later, only now, in the attempt to locate a self, a place.

Like others of that savage tribe I moved and lived with, along with them, I tortured gophers, scattered and smashed the huge co-operatives that ants built on the prairies, studied their wars, their cities, sucked wild onions and soured my mouth in chokecherries, masturbated in gangs, peered up the back of two-seaters in some wild scatological hope, pored over the corset ads in the Eaton's catalogue, all in the sweaty, thick closeness of the childhood dream. But if culture and nature were then hopelessly at odds, another division soon appeared as well, a rift within culture itself. I suppose its first manifestation was through radio: the language describing the Primo Carnero—Max Baer heavyweight championship fight. Somehow I knew the whole of Jewish prairie culture was at stake in that collosally inept struggle. And other voices in other rooms: Eddie Cantor, Lil Orphan Annie, secret codes, impossible adventures. Somewhere Graham Greene talks about his lost childhood, how it is that at one moment, one book *becomes* a metaphor of your own life, in some way perhaps even a determinant. Your dreams and images live out your life and though you never do become the heroic figure of *The Viper of Milan* (Greene's own fateful choice of books) or even the villain in that work, you act out the metaphors by your reticence, your evasions, your commitments, perhaps if you are lucky enough or obsessed enough, in the forms of your own imagination.

Alongside *Elbert Hubbard's Scrap Book* and its pernicious poems another book appears, this one of my own choosing, though try as I will, I can't recall how it came into my hands. What I do know is that once I began to read it, nothing could take me from it and that I would do anything to find the money to get another of the series. Elbert Hubbard could be read to me, but I would lie, cheat, steal, betray, do anything to be able to read another issue of *Doc Savage:*

> The golden man stood strangely silent at the edge of his laboratory table. For a long while he studied the object under the crystal, his pale eyes flickering, gold flecks swirling oddly in them. At last he spoke to the ape-like figure beside him. 'Monk' he said, 'what is it?' One huge hairy arm gestured. The world's leading organic chemist looked over to his companion. 'I don't know' he said.

Northrop Frye, whose name is bound to come up in this discussion sooner or later, calls stories like those in *Doc Savage* romances and tends to talk of them as more or less pure versions of story, that is, form or imagination. "Form," he says, "becomes something more like the shaping spirit, the power of ordering which seems so mysterious to the poet himself, because it often acts as though it were an identity separate from him. What corresponds to content is the sense of otherness, the resistance of the material, the feeling that there is something to be overcome, or at least struggled with." As a theory, I suppose it is as good as any. For what I have been talking about is the shaping form and the sense of otherness, the resistant material. What isn't clear is whether the prairies themselves are a form that imposes itself on the resistant self or whether it goes the other way around: we possess these stories, not even our own, and try to put their shapes on a world which resists fiercely.

One last personal allusion and some remarks on contemporary poets and I will be through. In the summer of 1973, Ann and I stopped, on the road to Wood Mountain, some forty miles past Estevan, to which we had returned, at the Jewish ghost town of Hoffer, Saskatchewan, the remnants of a Jewish colony with which my family has remote connections. There's some dispute about its status. I've been told the real name is Sonnenfeld and it is still being farmed. But on that hot July 1st, as I stood looking at the traces of some fifty or sixty years of life—a door frame still standing, an iron bedstead and Quebec stove resting in the grass, two or three sheds, a shell of a house, a huge concrete vault, the colonies' papers still there on the damp dirt floor—I was possessed not only by a troubling sense of transience, lost hopes, small human marks on a vast landscape, my own past disappearing, but by a question that had slowly been forming itself in my mind for the whole summer. Would this mute, intransigent place ever say anything? Was the only language one I imposed or whatever impelled my own speech? What *would* Doc Savage do in a crisis of these dimensions?

The answer, of course, was right there before me—and it constitutes everything I have been trying to say in the paper. The writer's subject *is* his own dilemma, writing west. For myself, it is the impossible divisions of gentility, vulgarity, Judaism, romance; a mixture not unlike the one (with some variations) you can find in Alice Munro writing about her childhood in Wingham, Ontario. Or in its poetic form, again with variations, in Suknaski's "West Central Pub":

> we smoke white owl cigars
> and drink white wine—
> john moneo says:
> lil jimmy rogers—
> now he made some fine lil records
> the lil bugger could sure sing—
> was a fine poet
> (they'll never touch him
> in a thousand years)

a young buck we know
walks in with a girl
none of us have ever seen—
moneo quotes service:
there are strange things done
in the midnight sun . . .
                    of wood mountain

adds lee soparlo

then a man from kildeer enters
wearing a pair of pants
that seem nothing but seams and patches—
i remark to john and lee:
in first year university
if you take philosophy
the dizzy fuckers talk about an ole ship—
the boards are replaced board by board
till a question plagues the mind—
is the ole ship there anymore—
at what point does the new ship
replace the old one?
then i talk about those pants
with patches seeming three layers deep—
wonder if we ever become something else
completely changed

the man with patched pants has overheard me
and asks:
where the fuck did you get your education?

i guess it begins now
i reply

The poem is about identity, change, process, the poet. And it deploys with beautiful subtlety several prairie motifs: the beer-drinking or wine-drinking philosophers; the beer-parlour as seminar and place of initiation; the poem as parody. But it also locates the poet for us in a striking use of an old image out of Gilbert & Sullivan: a thing of rags and patches, the wandering minstrel, ineffectual lover and singer, prince in disguise. And it's that sense of identity or patchwork, a *now* patched up of *then* and no longer the same, that gives Suknaski's work its authenticity. Al Purdy, in his introduction to the poems, says rightly, "This book is in no sense a history of the area, although it does deal with Wood Mountain people and history. Nor is it an autobiography of Andy Suknaski, although his own life is both marginally and centrally involved." For Purdy that means the book gives us, as he says, "a clear look at people and places," and exploration of the territory of time, a sense of place unequalled anywhere else, an overriding sense of sadness, and nostalgia and affection as well. Fair enough. No one, I think, in this country is more sensitive to voice and tone in poetry than Purdy, in his own poetry, in his critical remarks. And he means only to introduce the book briefly. What I

75

hear in Suknaski's work differs from Purdy's version only in emphasis, I
think. Purdy chooses the metaphor of territory or place for time, the
double sense of time in Suknaski's poems. Place, then, is in Purdy's
phrase "Multi-dimensional" so that whatever a clear look at place means,
it is by no means a simple matter. To change the metaphor, if *Wood
Mountains Poems* is about roots at all, these are a tangled and complicated
mass, and more than anything else, it is the poet's unease, his deep-
rooted embarrassment, as he touches on, reveals, the tangle, that comes
through to us—not sadness, not nostalgia, not affection, but shame,
everything implied in his own use of words like "betrayal" and "guilt".

I don't know how one describes an art of embarrassment. There's a
moment in Alice Munro's *Dance of the Happy Shades* when a vulgarly
refined group of middle-class ladies suffer excrutiatingly because they
have to sit through a recital played by idiot children. And Munro doesn't
let us off the hook easily. The idiot child plays effortlessly "something
fragile, courtly, and gay, that carries with it the freedom of a great
unemotional happiness." How can that be? "What do you write?" she is
asked; "Fiction" she replies, and she goes on "Bearing my humiliation by
this time with ease."

Nostalgia, sadness, memory, even affection—these are not difficult,
nor are they necessarily the source of poetic power. Language and form
are other matters.

As Purdy says, "There is nothing flashy or sensational" about *Wood
Mountain Poems*, "no verbal surprises or gymnastics (apart from the elas-
ticity of time)" but there is an exceptional sense of dialect, of voice, as if
Suknaski were hearing sounds carried by the wind: fragment of speech,
the way it *sounded* to be there, what was said. Why *that* is important I leave
it to you to sort out, but it is true that wherever the diction of poetry radically alters, unusual things are happening, both in sensibility and culture.

> *geez*
> *all the time slim/ting*

says Jimmie Hoy in one of Suknaski's poems; Hoy, owner of an archetyp-
al, mythical real Chinese Cafe, an immortal prairie place:

> *all time talkie too much*
> *makie trouble summa bitch*
> *wadda hell madder wid you?*
> *geez clyz*
> *all time slim thing*

Voices, like Johnny Nicholson's grandfather: "Johnny . . . hiss too cold
here in Siniboia/hiss be different from Wood Mountain/i think mehbee
me n babah . . . vee go back to farm in spring/orr mehbee propperty in
mooz jow." Or the modulation from Ukrainian to Yiddish English, the
old Jew commenting on furs he is bringing: "deez one is primarry/deez

76

one is ordinary/and deez one is jewst a fooking doog" or to native speech: "before I beg/I will cut willows for my young men to use/while killing mice to survive," or most chilling of all, a father's words in that incredible opening poem "Homestead": "When these things happen to me/do all you can and help one another save yourselves/from me."

The last words speak, to me at least, of a profound sense of betrayal in the word itself. After all, how and why should we turn others, especially those closest to ourselves, into poetry, as Suknaski does in the confessions of "Homestead"? Why write and re-write the past? It's always the past. Why relive the "unbearable moment" of recognition?

On the road to Wood Mountain, we saw petroglyphs, signs carved into the rock. Long ago men wrote pictures and words into the land. A curious impulse. It seemed to me then when I saw those, as now, that like the lost home of Estevan, the lost language of the petroglyphs were definitions of the prairie and that it would be in the voice of poets we would hear those definitions again. Divided men seeking to make themselves whole. Men out of place here—or anywhere. Andy Suknaski writes:

> leaving home having arrived
> at the last of all follies
> believing something here was mine
> believing i could return
> and build a home
> within the dying
>
> leaving home and shugmanitou
> the cry of the hounds
> drawing nearer

NOTES

1. W.H. New's *Articulating West* informs more than the title, and a comment in Ann Mandel's "The Frontiers of Memory" in *The Laurentian Review* provided the necessary memories and form.

2. Compare the Kipling quotation from Hubbard with these lines from a song composed in 1932 about the Estevan strike.

> In a little mining village
> Scarcely noticed on the map
> Bourgeois guns were turned on workers
> And their life's blood there did sap.
>
> No one dreamed of such a slaughter
> In that town of Estevan,
> That armed thugs with guns and bullets
> Would shoot men with empty hands.
>
> Just a protest from the miners,
> And boss bullets then did fly,

Caring not who was the target
Or the number that would die.

Blazing forth, nine hundred bullets
Bodies full of lead did fill,
Murdered three, and wounded twenty—
But the Cause they could not kill.

Three more martyrs for the miners,
Three more murders for the boss
Brutal laws, to crush the workers
Who dare fight in Freedom's cause.

As those miners lay a-dying
In their agony and pain,
Whispered, "Though we die for freedom,
Yet we do not die in vain."

The song entitled, "Estevan," appeared on p. 2 of the *Canadian Miner*, published in Calgary January 30, 1932. The lyrics were composed by
Cecil Boone and the tune is that of the old Irish Rebel song, "Kevin Barry."
The song is quoted in *Towards a New Past*, "An Oral History of Industrial Unrest in the Estevan—Bienfait Coalfields." Department of Culture and Youth, Government of Saskatchewan, p. 47.

III
Writers and Writing

Modern
Canadian
Poetry

The difficulty in writing about a modern movement in Canadian poetry is that many of its concerns appear to be local and national in a world in which, as Northrop Frye observes, "the nation is rapidly ceasing to be the real defining unit of society."[1] Obviously, the view that we are now "moving towards a post-national world"[2] makes more cultural than political or social sense, though it is for that reason that the contemporary arts seem more closely connected with revolutionary attitudes than with traditional values. It is this revolutionary aspect of the " 'modern' element in the culture of the last century"[3] that occupies Frye in *The Modern Century*. Considered as style, the modern exhibits characteristically anarchic features: deliberate fragmenting of literary form, either through disorder or parody; irrationalism; disruption or inversion of value systems; and disoriented versions of perception. In turn, radicalism of style connects with radical, anarchic social (or anti-social) attitudes, particularly in what Frye calls a Freudian proletarianism that seeks to overthrow through pornography or sexual assault the repressive anxiety-structure of society. What is modern in Canadian poetry, then, we would want to connect with aspects of radicalism in its style and attitude. What, in fact, we appear to be left with, as a sort of national residue, is that which seems impossible to reconcile with radicalism in our poetry: its nostalgia, its longing for history, its impulse to define a Canadian past and to create a usable tradition.

On the whole, the sort of criticism which sees poetry as a reflection of environment simply resorts to any one of a number of dualisms to explain this apparent contradiction of the local and international in Canadian writing. Occasionally, we hear of the tension in Canadian life between vulgarity and daintiness. There are other, familiar pairs: American and British influences on Canadian poetry; realism and formalism; colonialism and nationalism; originality and imitativeness. Projected as a genuine rift in Canadian life, dualism becomes the ultimate secret, what

81

Malcolm Ross speaks of as "the broad design of our unique, inevitable, and precarious cultural pattern." "This pattern, by the force of historical and geographical circumstances," Ross goes on to say, "is a pattern of opposites in tension . . . the federal-regional tension . . . the American-British tension . . . the French-English tension."[4]

If Ross's is an extreme version of dualism in Canadian life, it at least has the merit of defining one limit of our discussion: poetry dissolves into the dualities of space and time. But time and space (or history and geography) can be resolved into poetry, perhaps at another extreme limit. Seen as sociology, contemporary poetry seems to reflect or project the duality of a Canadian stereotype at once reticent, conservative, modest *and* radical, ill-mannered, and visionary. The split, unbelievable at best, obviously dresses up in national clothing the familiar division of poetry into form and content. Local and quaint in the content of its rock-bound historicism, Canadian poetry still manages to be modishly perceptive in its sophisticated techniques. Whatever that division might mean, it disappears the moment we become aware that time and space may present themselves, not as sociology, but as myth.

It is not by the way to notice that for the most part myth criticism concerns itself with questions of national and cultural identity, or with the *distinctiveness* of the Canadian imagination. Where, as in Frye's comments, the mythic appears as a formal, and therefore autonomous, element in poetry, we find something closer to genuine cultural history, and his perception that with the Confederation poets, particularly Carman, myth developed out of romantic impressionism, provides a vital clue to what can be seen as the modern element in Canadian poetry. It is, paradoxically, in the longing for history that the modern appears, for out of that longing emerge finally both the hallucinated terror and the diminished self of contemporary art.

When the poet seeks to discover life in a threatening landscape and to create a usable past, both space and time tend to become esoteric, exotic, and ultimately primitive. Certainly, as often as not in modern Canadian poetry, "the orient eye decides geography," a place remote from the poet's "natural country." So it is that Earle Birney turns up in Mexico, in South America, in Japan, in India; and Al Purdy, with suit-case full of wine bottles, sends his messages from Cuba or Baffin-Land or Greece; Leonard Cohen journeys to and from Montreal, to Hydra, and, "the only tourist," sends poems from Havana to Canada, while Irving Layton discovers allegories of poet and critic in elephants and trees in Ceylon, or comments on sun-bathers, politicians, poets and lizards in Portugal, Spain, Greece, and Israel. Nor are these simply the jottings of the poet as tourist, a Canadian version of the Fulbright Fellow. Often the suggestion is that the "foreign" space discovered bears its symbolic freight of time, history, and culture. For Birney and Purdy, in particular, the past or distant place speaks as a metaphor of the present and the familiar.

Occasionally, the image of a journey or of distance reflects the perception of those for whom emptiness has for too long been a burden. For some, then, space becomes strict, northern, barren, as in F.R. Scott's Laurentian poems, Birney's arctic and west-coast poems, and Purdy's Baffin-Land poems. For others, it becomes overtly symbolic, as in Gwen MacEwen's "The Discovery":

> do not imagine that the exploration
> ends, that she has yielded all her mystery
> or that the map you hold
> cancels further discovery
>
> I tell you her uncovering takes years,
> takes centuries, and when you find her naked
> look again,
> admit there is something else you cannot name,
> a veil, a coating just above the flesh
> which you cannot remove by your mere wish
>
> when you see the land naked, look again
> (burn your maps, that is not what I mean),
> I mean the moment when it seems most plain
> is the moment when you must begin again.[5]

The place the poet occupies may be that curious one implied by Margaret Avison's extraordinary "Meeting Together of Poles & Latitudes: in Prospect," or it may be "the land the passionate man must travel," in Douglas Le Pan's "Country Without a Mythology," or "the desperate wilderness behind your eyes," in his "Coureurs de bois." For P.K. Page, it seems to be somewhere "behind the eyes / where silent, unrefractive whiteness lies," while for Margaret Atwood it is either "the mind's deadend, the roar of the boneyard" reached during the night in the Royal Ontario Museum or that incredible landscape, a deluge of unstructured space, in "Progressive Insanities of a Pioneer."[6]

Atwood's mad pioneer brings us, as it were, to our senses: "It is," as Charles Olson says in a famous essay, "a matter, finally, of OBJECTS, what they are, what they are inside a poem, how they got there, and, once there, how they are to be used."[7] The creation of a usable past is the creation of a mythology, or in Olson's version, ". . . a man's problem, the moment he takes speech up in all its fullness, is to give his work his seriousness, a seriousness sufficient to cause the thing he makes to try to take its place alongside the things of nature."[8] Like the mad pioneer, we must expect strange things to happen to space and time. As Margaret Atwood puts it in her poem "Astral Traveller":

> Here the sense
> of time used to no
> gravity, warps
> in the old atmosphere.

In the same poem she suggests that "Getting away was easy" but "Coming back is an exacting theory." The "exacting theory" of her poem involves the problem of getting back into one's own body. For the Canadian poet the problem is how to handle the space-time warp of "the old atmosphere." Like astronauts in zero gravity, the poets find themselves involved in those contortions needed to resolve the paradoxes of "then" that is "now", and "there" that is "here." In Al Purdy's "Wilderness Gothic", for example, "gothic ancestors peer from medieval sky" somewhere just beyond Toronto at Roblin Lake. Birney's "El Greco: *Espolio*" plays ironically with a many-layered time: a contemporary version of a sixteenth-century painter's version of a crucifixion scene. Arched into the gothic forms of cathedral, the wilderness of Emily Carr's painting turns into the inverted whale-boat church that, in Wilfred Watson's poem, takes the painter as a kind of Jonah back through the wilderness itself to be cast out onto the "coasts of eternity" where, as poet addresses painter, the final transformations work themselves into an ancient language:

> Then, as for John of Patmos, the river of life
> Burned for you an emerald and jasper smoke
> And down the valley you looked and saw
> All wilderness become transparent vapour,
> A ghostly underneath a fleshly stroke,
> And every bush an apocalypse of leaf[9]

But if the wilderness for Watson reveals itself as Biblical vision, for Birney it is just as likely to sound in the voices of Anglo-Saxon bards (as in "Vancouver Lights" or "Mappemounde") and for Purdy in the sound of more ancient singers:

> Brother, the wind of this place is cold,
> And hills under our feet tremble,
> the forests are making magic against us—
> I think the land knows we are here,
> I think the land knows we are strangers.
> Let us stay close to our friend the sea,
> or cunning dwarves at the roots of darkness
> shall seize and drag us down. . . .
>
> Brother, I am afraid of this dark place,
> I am hungry for the home islands,
> And wind blowing the waves to coloured spray,
> I am sick for the sun—[10]

The lines are from Purdy's poem "The Runners", the epigraph to which is a striking passage from Erick the Red's Saga. It is worth quoting in full in order to elicit from it not only its remarkable sense that the primitive illuminates and comments on the contemporary but equally its capacity to create a powerfully surrealistic context of tensions between widely

differing scales of value. The effect is not unlike that in Cavafy's remarkable poem "Expecting the Barbarians":

> It was when Lief was with King Olaf Tryggvason, and he bade him
> proclaim Christianity to Greenland, that the King gave him two
>   Gaels;
> the man's name was Haki, and the woman's Haekia. The kin
>   advised
> Lief to have recourse to these people, if he should stand in need of
> fleetness, for they were swifter than deer. Erick and Lief had
>   tendered
> Karlsefni the services of this couple. Now when they had sailed past
> Marvel-Strands (to the New World) they put the Gaels ashore, and
> directed them to run to the southward, and investigate the nature
>   of the
> country, and return again before the end of the third half-day.

What we have been observing to this point is how that which appears
as the Canadian writer's conservatism (his nostalgia, his longing for
history, his impulse to define the past and a usable tradition) becomes,
almost as it were by law, not only myth, but theory of myth; a vision not
only of the primitive, but of the sources of the primitive. Creating its
own space and time, a mythic geography reveals the mask of imagination, a primitive blood-streaked face. In John Newlove's "The Pride", the
poet thinks of all the great mythic masks and stories of the tribes.
Meditating on "This western country crammed/with the ghosts of indians," he asks,

> But what image, bewildered
> son of all men
> under the hot sun,
> do you worship,
> what completeness
> do you hope to have
> from these tales. . . .

And the answer begins to form as he calls to mind the past. History is a
nightmare of blood and battle:

> in summer and in the bloody fall
> they gathered on the killing grounds,
> fat and shining with fat, amused
> with the luxuries of war and death,
>
> relieved from the stream of knowledge,
> consoled by the stream of blood
> and steam rising from the fresh hides
> and tired horses, wheeling in their pride
> on the sweating horses, their pride.

But if history is blood, imagination too is blood-soaked. Place, event, and
poem are so interfused, it is not possible to tell one from the other:
"Those are all stories;/the pride, the grand poem/of our land, of the earth

itself," a poem like "the sunlit brilliant image" that "suddenly floods us/with understanding shocks our/attention." For the contemporary poet, the identification is complete: "at last we become them/in our desires, our desires."[11]

The longing for history appears finally, as in Newlove's poem, as an image of primitive desire, the imaginative source of poetry. But in what sense can this be said to be either modern or radical? There are two possibilities. One is suggested by a comment of Fiedler's, another by Charles Olson.

Concerned to develop his argument that the return of the primitive in "the new western" involves what he speaks of as "the alteration of consciousness," Fiedler notices, "the real opposite of nostalgic is psychedelic, the reverse of remembering is hallucinating."[12] The point at issue is not to invoke Fiedler's own version of redskins and palefaces, but to remind ourselves of the connection between primitive and contemporary modes in poetry. At its extreme limit, the mythology of space and time turns into a myth of primitive hallucination. The progressive insanities of a pioneer "transmute memory into madness, dead legend into living hallucination."[13] Among contemporary poets, the most striking manifestation of the return of the primitive as hallucination, of course, is Cohen's *Beautiful Losers*, but something of the same process can be seen in the phonemic tantras of B.P. Nichol, in the concretism of Joe Rosenblatt, and in Bill Bissett's visionary chants and ideograms.[14] And as Cohen's invocation to "Alexander Trocchi, Public Junkie" reminds us, the myth of hallucination involves more than poetry as madness. Its context may very well be McLuhan's tribalization, or it may involve what Frye speaks of as a sadistic withdrawal from society in the linking of criminality and art, in addition to the pastoral withdrawal in the communal idea of freedom and spontaneity. Whatever its specific form, the Canadian version of hallucinated terror and freedom obviously depends more heavily on contemporary literary conventions than on some nebulous version of Canadian character or local culture. Gary Snyder and Allan Ginsberg are clearly more pertinent to the themes we are concerned with here than, say, the Social Credit or the Toronto-Dominion Centre. Modern poetry is international in style and radical in its attitudes; that is to say, it is fundamentally anti-social in its manic, sadistic, and pastoral concerns. To the extent that Canadian poets share not only this international style but the radicalism of their contemporaries, we can speak of them as modern poets.

But there is another sense in which the myth of space and time may be said to be modern, and though in some ways it is less extreme than the terrorist side of the pattern, it suggests even more important possibilities. Attempting to work out "the degree to which the projective involves a stance toward reality outside a poem as well as a new stance towards the reality of a poem itself," Charles Olson is led to comment on what he speaks of as "objectism":

> Objectism is the getting rid of the lyrical interference of the individual as ego, of the 'subject' and his soul, that peculiar presumption by which western man has interposed himself between what he is as a creature of nature (with certain instructions to carry out) and those other creations of nature which we may, with no derogation, call objects.... It comes to this: the use of a man, by himself and thus by others, lies in how he conceives his relation to nature, that force to which he owes his somewhat small existence. If he sprawl, he shall find little to sing but himself, and shall sing, nature has such paradoxical ways, by way of artificial forms outside himself. But if he stays inside himself, if he is contained within his nature as he is participant in the larger force, he will be able to listen, and his hearing through himself will give him secrets objects share.[15]

For obvious reasons, Olson's statement belongs here, most patently because of his influence on a group of poets writing from Vancouver: Frank Davey, Lionel Kearns, and George Bowering, among others. A more serious consideration is Olson's redefinition of the role of ego and the place and meaning of perception in poetry. Historically, it has been argued, myth develops as a psychologizing of romantic impressionism. As a narrative of contending powers of the psyche, it objectifies the self in cultural history and nature. So, at least for some time, myth was understood (at least according to rumour) by such poets as Douglas Le Pan, Wilfred Watson, Anne Wilkinson, and Daryl Hine, and so it was presented (more or less programmatically) by James Reaney and Jay Macpherson. No one is likely to deny Miss Macpherson's achievement in *The Boatman,* still the most beautifully coherent and lyrical book of recent years. Nor should Watson's and Reaney's contribution to poetic drama be ignored. But Olson's poetic opened the way to a radically different approach to the myth of emptiness in space. Instead of "singing himself and singing by way of artificial forms outside himself," that is, by way of the imposed design of psyche and story, the poet opens himself to the language of objects and their secrets. Whatever one makes of the theory, in practice its impact could scarcely be ignored.

The laconic comes to be favoured over the elaborated structure; the unemphatic tone seems more precise than the singing voice in dramatic or ironic lyrics; the poem as experience, apparently extemporized, is preferable to the poem as literature, a structure set apart for contemplation. And while it is virtually impossible to see any extensive body of work as solely the product or character of one pattern in poetry, it seems clear enough that Ray Souster's continued concern with the observed object or process of perception, on the one hand, and Al Purdy's curious brand of psychological realism, on the other, have assumed a more significant role in the development of contemporary poetry than, say, the more dramatic and flamboyant assertiveness of Irving Layton's

work. The poets represented in Souster's anthology *New Wave: Canada*
speak variously. Michael Ondaatje's elegantly controlled world of "slight,
careful stepping birds," "parrots and appalled lions," is not likely to be
mistaken for Victor Coleman's quiet measures. But it is openness and
"objectism" that dominate in the anthology, as they dominate still in so
influential a contemporary magazine as David Rosenberg's *The Ant's
Forefoot.*[16] With *New Wave: Canada,* in fact, the shift away from psychological myth to the myth of the object is virtually complete, and the "open-
ended" poem of process and perception replaces closed structure and
"literary" form.

Souster dedicates his anthology "To W.W.E. Ross, the first modern
Canadian poet," and in his brief preface, the book intends to mark a sharp
revaluation of contemporary developments. Where it had long been
maintained that the modern movement in Canada begins with the witty,
complex, socially aware poetry of A.J.M. Smith, F.R. Scott, and A.M.
Klein, and the vigorous narratives of E.J. Pratt, from the point of view of
writers like Souster, Purdy, and the *New Wave* poets, the contemporary
begins with Ross, Dorothy Livesay, and Raymond Knister. At a glance,
the difference between the two groups appears to be in the influences
upon them, the one group responding to Eliot, Yeats, and Auden, the
other to the American imagists, Pound, Williams, and Olson. But more
important than a reassessment of literary influences, the revaluation of
the past implies a change in sensibility and vision. As Bowering puts it in
his "Bright Land": "What gives it to you . . . your eyes . . . as in the old
literature," but "It is, as I've said, your approach/does it."[17]

Space finally comes to be occupied not by legend but by objects. And at
this point, the terror of emptiness recedes. The spiritual project of
humanizing the wilderness and of creating a usable past paradoxically
turns itself inside out.[18] It reaches completeness with its realization of
the object and its acceptance of what is there. One is reminded of the
terrific ironic force in Robbe-Grillet's remarks: "if I say, 'The world is
man,' I shall always gain absolution; while if I say, 'Things are things, and
man is only man,' I am immediately charged with a crime against humanity."[19] There is a literature for which Robbe-Grillet's comments are
appropriate, the anti-arts of Mailer and Genet, the silences of Beckett
and Pinter, the randomness of Burroughs, a parodic universe of chance,
change, magic, occultism. Its end is silence, as Susan Sontag under-
stands: "From the promotion of the arts into 'art' comes the leading myth
about art, that of the absoluteness of the artist's activity. . . . The later
version of the myth posits a more complex, tragic relation of art to
consciousness. . . . Art is not consciousness per se, but rather its antidote. . . ."[20] In brief, "the pursuit of silence." It seems possible to claim
that where we find a poetry which substitutes "chance for intention,"
where magic is afoot and "Art is the enemy of the artist," we find a poetry
that seeks the same renewal or renunciation that informs so much con-

temporary writing. At the very least, we might notice that the narrative hero of *Beautiful Losers* dissolves in the last pages of his book into a radio, a giant cinema image, and finally nothingness: "His presence was like the shape of an hour glass, strongest where it was smallest." The "feature of the evening," we are told, according to some purists, is "this point of most absence."[21] It is a point, we might believe, from which anything could begin.

NOTES

1. Northrop Frye, *The Modern Century* (Toronto: Oxford, 1967), p. 18.

2. Frye, p. 17.

3. Frye, p. 57.

4. *Poets of the Confederation*, ed. Malcolm Ross (Toronto: McClelland and Stewart, 1960), p. xi.

5. Gwendolyn MacEwen, *The Shadow-Maker* (Toronto: Macmillan, 1969), p. 30. Referred to here as well are Earle Birney, *Selected Poems* (Toronto: McClelland and Stewart, 1966); A.W. Purdy, *Wild Grape Wine* (Toronto: McClelland and Stewart, 1968), and *North of Summer* (Toronto: McClelland and Stewart, 1967); Leonard Cohen, *Selected Poems* (Toronto: McClelland and Stewart, 1968); Irving Layton, *Collected Poems* (Toronto: McClelland and Stewart, 1965); F.R. Scott, *Selected Poems* (Toronto: Oxford, 1966).

6. Margaret Atwood, *The Animals in That Country* (Toronto: Oxford, 1968); P.K. Page, *Cry Ararat* (Toronto: McClelland and Stewart, 1967); Douglas Le Pan, *The Wounded Prince* (London: Chatto and Windus, 1948); Margaret Avison, *Winter Sun* (Toronto: University of Toronto, 1960).

7. Charles Olson, "Projective Verse", *Human Universe and Other Essays*, ed. Donald Allen (New York: Grove Press, 1967), pp. 55-56.

8. Olson, p. 60.

9. Wilfred Watson, *Friday's Child* (London: Faber and Faber, 1955), p. 55.

10. A.W. Purdy, *Wild Grape Wine* (Toronto: McClelland and Stewart, 1968), p. 110.

11. John Newlove, *Black Night Window* (Toronto: McClelland and Stewart, 1968), pp. 105 ff.

12. Leslie Fiedler, *The Return of the Vanishing American* (New York: Stein and Day, 1968), p. 175.

13. Fiedler, pp. 176-177.

14. Leonard Cohen, *Beautiful Losers* (Toronto: McClelland and Stewart, 1966); bp Nichol, *Journeyings and the Return* (Toronto: Coach House Press, 1967); Joe Rosenblatt, *Winter of the Luna Moth* (Toronto: House of Anansi, 1968); Bill Bissett, *Of The Land Divine Service* (Toronto: Weed/Flower Press, 1968), and *Lebanon Voices* (Toronto: Weed/Flower Press, 1967).

15. Olson, pp. 59-60.

16. *The Ant's Forefoot*, ed. D. Rosenberg (Toronto: Coach House Press); *New Wave: Canada*, ed. Raymound Souster, (Toronto: Contact Press, 1967); Souster's own work should be looked at in *The Colour of the Times* (Toronto: Ryerson,

1964), *As Is* (Toronto: Oxford, 1967), and *Lost and Found* (Toronto: Clarke, Irwin, 1968); Anne Wilkinson, *The Collected Poems of Anne Wilkinson*, ed. A.J.M. Smith (Toronto: Macmillan, 1968); Jay Macpherson, *The Boatman* (Toronto: Oxford, 1968); James Reaney, *Twelve Letters to a Small Town* (Toronto: Ryerson, 1962); Daryl Hine, *The Wooden Horse* (New York: Atheneum 1965).

17. *Thumbprints*, ed. Doug Fetherling (Toronto: Peter Martin Associates, 1969), p. 13. See also George Bowering, *Rocky Mountain Foot* (Toronto: McClelland and Stewart, 1968); W.W.E. Ross, *Shapes and Sounds* (Toronto: Longman's 1968); Dorothy Livesay, *The Documentaries* (Toronto: Ryerson, 1968); and *Day and Night* (Toronto: Ryerson, 1944); Raymond Knister, *The Collected Poems of Raymond Knister* (Toronto: Ryerson, 1949); A.J.M. Smith, *Poems: New and Collected* (Toronto: Oxford, 1967); A.M. Klein, *Hath Not a Jew* (New York: Ryerson, 1940), and *The Rocking Chair and Other Poems* (Toronto: Ryerson, 1948); E.J. Pratt, *Collected Poems* (Toronto: Macmillan, 1958).

18. Northrop Frye, "Letters, In Canada: Poetry, 1952-1960," in *Masks of Poetry*, ed. A.J. M. Smith (Toronto: McClelland and Stewart, 1962).

19. Alain Robbe-Grillet, "Nature, Humanism, Tragedy", in *For a New Novel* (New York: Grove Press, 1965), p. 52.

20. Susan Sontag, "The Aesthetics of Silence", in *Styles of Radical Will* (New York: Farrar, Straus and Giroux, 1969), p. 4.

21. Cohen, *Beautiful Losers*, pp. 241-242.

Ethnic Voice
in
Canadian Writing

To begin with a dilemma. Any entry into the sociology of writing offers genuine theoretical difficulties, and yet the subject to which I have been asked to address myself calls for just such an entry. Of course, you might ask: why not simply be satisfied with description and simple categorization? The answer, I think, is that, in some way, the subject of ethnicity generates pressures that do not permit anything like the remoteness suggested by an easy survey. At this point, it seems to me, the real alternatives become clear: the material before me, the subject itself, is either fictional or not. I mean precisely to question the subject itself, to ask where is the source of this deep-rooted and troublesome sense that somehow it is always evading us, slipping away. Let me illustrate.

"The true meaning of *immigrant* is . . . to be dispossessed of the culture even if one is born into it," remarks Elizabeth Janeway.[1] "We are all immigrants to this place," says Margaret Atwood.[2] "Well, yes," we say. But when she adds that we're all mental patients too, our agreement may not come so easily. Quite possibly it is only Atwood's habit of mind that leads her to see the spirit of this country as a ghostly mad old woman on a St. Clair street car or that moves her to work out all the implications in the image of *alien:* to feel in that word not only a sense of *otherness,* of being apart from, foreign, but even more, a sense of the *un-natural,* as in the science-fiction sense of the word. Or could it be that a disturbing, dislocating quality enters the discussion the moment we place concepts of social class, cultural definition, or group structure at the forefront? It is not only that as strangers we find ourselves in a strange land, but with the burden upon us as well, to paraphrase a remark of M.L. Lautt's, of living simultaneously within the influences of our own and another's culture.[3] To live in doubleness, that is difficult enough. To articulate that doubleness simply intensifies the pressure, the burden. But there is a further step in which what Atwood calls "inescapable doubleness" turns into duplicity, a strategy for cultural identification that I take to be the ethnic strategy, the "voice" I'm trying to identify in these remarks. The sense in which I am using the term "duplicitous" is perhaps special, though I hope it will become clear enough from the examples I have chosen, as well as from a general comment on the senses in which we can speak of the "self" as deceptive. The comment is R.D. Laing's. The examples, from what we usually call ethnic writing, are not extensive, and the questions which then arise I will want to face after having said what I can about the writers and works I choose here.

First, then, Laing's comment:

> Heidegger . . . has contrasted the natural scientific concept of truth with a notion of truth which has its origins in pre-Socratic thinking. Whereas in natural science truth consists in a correspondence, an adequatio, between what goes on *in intellectu* and what goes on *in re,* between the structure of a symbol system 'in the mind' and the structure of events 'in the world,' there is another concept of truth which is to be found in the Greek word *Alethaia.* In this concept, truth is literally that which is without secrecy, what discloses itself without being veiled. . . . When one sees actions of the other in the light of this latter form of truth or falsehood, one says that a man is truthful or 'true to himself' when one 'feels' that he means what he says, or is saying what he means. . . . Between such 'truth' and a lie there is room for the most curious and subtle ambiguities and complexities in the person's disclosure/concealment of himself. . . . What has been revealed, what concealed, and to whom, in the Gioconda smile, in the 'twixt earnest and joke' of Blake's angel, in the infinite pathos—or is it apathy—of a Harlequin of Picasso. The liar (he deceives others without deceiving himself), the hysteric (his deception of himself is anterior to his deception of others), the actor (*his* actions are not 'him'), the hypocrite, the imposter (like Thomas Mann's Felix Krull, absorbed into the parts he plays), are at the one time the exploiters and victims of the almost unlimited possibilities in the self's relation to its own acts, and of the lack of final assurance that one can attribute correctly the other's relation to his actions.[4]

The landscape we enter in ethnic culture, then, is not so much social as psychological, that problematic and perplexing place where we confront "the almost unlimited possibilities in the self's relation to its own acts." And the reason for this is surely not entirely mysterious. As soon as a question of ethnicity is raised, the question of identity appears along with it. A psychologist like Laing sees identity questions in phenomenological terms but accepts as well the accompanying paradox that while definitions abstract, the boundary-less world is schizophrenic. As Gloria Onley argues, Laing "seems to believe that schizophrenia is a form of psychic anarchy: a usually involuntary attempt by the self to free itself from a repressive social reality structure."[5] In critical and literary terms, this means what is only too evident in Canadian writing: to raise the question of identity is virtually to assure that it cannot be answered. I don't think it has been observed that part of the extra-ordinary power of

Atwood's *Survival*—and perhaps one reason for its enormous success—lies in her perception that the problem of identity can only be answered in fictional terms, that is, by turning it into a story. *Survival* is a ghost story disguised as politics and criticism. The victor/victim pattern enables Atwood to work out as Canada's identity a sado-masochistic sexual fantasy that is at the basis of gothic tales. Or to put this point another way, as another of our novelists, Robert Kroetsch does, "In a sense we haven't got an identity until somebody tells our story. The fiction makes us real."[6] As with the nation, then, so with its mosaic, its cultural identities, the ethnic voices to which I now turn.

II

I turn (I would say, naturally enough) to Jewish writers, Mordecai Richler, Leonard Cohen, Irving Layton. Shortly, I want to extend these remarks to include John Marlyn and F.P. Grove, and a number of poets whose work has been translated from their own languages into English. I suppose that much of what I have to say here—and elsewhere in this paper—is essentially an elaborate footnote to George Woodcock's comments in his fine book on Richler and particularly to this remark: "It might be a metaphorical exaggeration to describe Canada as a land of invisible ghettoes, but certainly it is, both historically and geographically, a country of minorities that have never achieved assimilation."[7] Whatever one makes of Richler's development from realism through farce to a peculiarly grotesque satiric mode, it is clear that thematically his concerns have remained constant, or if there is a development it involves simply a growing and deepening sense of what the question of identity implies or, more specifically, what is implied in the attempt to escape from the ghetto. In practice, this works out as a series of choices given in the novels, each novel moving toward a choice which then creates the situation for the next. *Choices* is perhaps the wrong word. Closer would be Sartre's whirligig: an opposition in which the opposing forces endlessly turn into one another and in which an endless oscillation between them appears to be the only mode of existence for the individual so trapped.

As often as not, Richler's whirligigs involve paradoxical inversions of identities: the Jew who is a goy; the goy who is a Jew, for example; in turn, these can be satirically or comically complicated by a reflexive series, such as the one that transforms a gentile into an anti-semitic Jew whose Jewishness is affirmed by the very vehemence of his denial of Jewishness. But there is a more sinister form as well: the man who is a monster, the monster who is man; and a whole series of related whirligigs spinning off from and commenting on the main ones: films creating reality; reality imitating films; barbarians who are civilized; cultivated barbarians, and so on. The generating force of the whirligigs is the structure of illusions that, for Richler, constitutes the ghetto or a community, nor is it by the way to notice how often such a community is culturally defined not by ethnicity, but by "creativity", that is, as a community of artists or film-makers or writers, always in Richler those who both manipulate illusion and who feed on social snobbishness. Richler's argument seems to me to be based on his conviction that class values (that is, economically determined positions) are more important to an individual's sense of self than are traditional values, a belief that economic rather than cultural forces define relationships, and equally that stereotypes are not only illusory but immoral.[8]

In practice, this argument, if it is one, dissolves into the forms and images of Richler's novels, but at the same time it does help explain some of the apparently gratuitous aspects of Richler's satire—he is never simply random or brutal—and it is the intellectual equivalent of the startling vision we now confront. *Son of a Smaller Hero,* for example, sets up what appears to be a resolution to an almost unbearable dilemma. If life in the ghetto is impossible because illusory, but to leave it is to be an other, not self, a denial of one's own existence, where then is home, how is authenitc *human* existence possible? Noah's decision not to define himself in opposition but by remaking himself, not by being a goy but a man, appears heroic, though everything that follows in Richler's work suggests it may be sinister. For the dialectic of self and other may generate not humanity, but monstrousness. Duddy Kravitz's ferocious energy turns him into Wonder-Boy, his own model of escape from the ghetto, Dingleman, and who *that* is, we see in a moment. The dialectic of *The Apprenticeship of Duddy Kravitz* is given to us in Uncle Benjy's letter. A great and terrible cry wells up in Benjy: "Experience doesn't teach; it deforms." But there is a footnote, "Be a Mensch."[9] The opposition surely is right. We now know what the choices are: deformity or menschlichkeit, the grotesque or the human. But Richler does not allow easy resolutions. The self-made, the re-made man Richler takes with terrifying literalness. He becomes the Star-Maker, the man with spare parts, plastic man, transplanted man, un-natural man, alien man, inhuman, androgynous, in George Woodcock's words, "a figure of nightmare, the monster lurching out of dreams and demanding to be clothed in modern guise who inhabits almost every Richler novel."[10]

"Be a Mensch" means re-make yourself. At the psychological level, that can mean, disastrously, to act like someone else, to turn into someone else. But in socio-cultural terms, the choice is scarcely better: the ghetto's conservatism opposed to society's liberalism, progress as physical transformation, transplantation. In moral terms, the great cry still is, as in Rilke: "There is no place that does not see you. You must change your life."[11] But, at least in Richler, the opposites, grotesque or human, resolve themselves monstrously. These choices obviously have been vigorously rejected by the Jewish community which regards Richler as a Jewish anti-semite. But the images he uses may be finally less horrifying then at first sight they appear.

In the binary oppositions of myth, Edmund R. Leach proposes the discriminations as between, say, "human/superhuman, mortal/immortal, male/female, legitimate/illegitimate, good/bad" despite "all variations of theology" remain constant and are "followed by a 'mediation' of the paired categories thus distinguished."[12]

He goes on to say:

> 'Mediation' (in this sense) is always achieved by introducing a third category which is 'abnormal' or 'anomalous' in terms of ordinary 'rational' categories. Thus myths are full of fabulous monsters, incarnate gods, virgin mothers. This middle ground is abnormal, non-natural, holy. It is typically the focus of all taboo and ritual observance.[13]

How can you be a Jew in a goyisha land? Be a monster. It is not so extraordinary, after all, though perhaps difficult to live with. The numinous figure *is* the resolution to an impossible situation, the situation of the ghetto, of ethnicity. To say this, is to say we are in the presence of a myth and all its duplicities. Leach, in the article from which I have quoted, argues, for example, the two major common characteristics of myth are redundancy and a markedly binary aspect; that is, myths tell the same story over and over again, and it always involves a dualism resolved by a monstrous or holy third. In the language of systems engineers "a high level of redundancy makes it easy to correct errors introduced by noise" or as Leach says "in the mind of the believer, myth does indeed convey messages which are the Word of God."[14] God, then, as systems engineer or computer operator, resolves dualities and reassures us daily, as Richler does, by telling again and again the same story of self, other, and monster.

My argument that the voice of ethnicity in literature is duplicitous turns out, after all, to look suspiciously like a form of structuralism. If so, it is only so to enable me to say, as Levi-Strauss does, in the introduction to *The Raw and the Cooked*, that we can only handle myths critically by writing them, that as I said earlier, stories of identity, though presented as social analyses and political propaganda, are ghost stories, or forms haunting our restless imagination. Ethnicity, I would argue, sets into motion for the writer a whirligig or duality that can only be resolved in a myth, a restructured self, a fictional being.

Take as another example Leonard Cohen's *Beautiful Losers*. Many have remarked on Cohen's preference for style over conviction, religiosity rather than religion, the quality that reminds one that a Montreal Jewish boy, as Pre-Raphaelite pretending to be mediaeval Catholic, convinced a whole generation of readers of the spirituality of his essentially perverse reading of Christianity. *Beautiful Losers*, it is fairly evident now, works out the whirligigs of male-female or female-male, by producing the monstrous tree-hermit Christ, a pederast, who turns into a movie. In Cohen's poetry, the sado-masochistic sense of sexuality prevails, coloured by a special elegance of phrase that does not conceal the profound polarity, Jewish-Christian, Master-Slave, that impels his work towards its fated end. By no accident, his latest book of poems appeals to us with another sexual version of ethnicity, *The Energy of Slaves*. Like William Burroughs, Cohen constructs or reconstructs selves in a sad narcotic exercise for numbing pain.

Layton's version of this myth essentially inverts both Cohen's and Richler's, attempting to insist the other is monstrous, the self authentic, Layton's self, of course, defined as identical to poet. Two observations here will suffice to take us through his version of ethnicity: one concerns his equating of poet with Jew and placing the Judaic-prophet-poet in opposition to WASP professor, presbyterian morality, Christian ethics and vision, Canadian society in its puritanical and lifeless routine, nowhere to better effect than in the stunning conclusion to his homage to Osip Mandelstaum:

> I know my fellow-Canadians, Osip;
> they forgot your name and fate as swiftly
> as they learned them, switching off
> the contorted image of pain with their sets,
> choosing a glass darkness to one which starting
> in the mind covers the earth in permanent eclipse;
> so they chew branflakes and crabmeat gossip make love
> take out insurance against fires and death
> while our poetesses explore their depressions
> in delicate complaints regular as menstruation
> or eviscerate a dead god for metaphors;
> the men-poets displaying codpieces of wampum,
> the safer legends of prairie Indian and Eskimo
>
> Under a sour and birdless heaven
> TV crosses stretch across a flat Calvary
> and plaza storewindows give me
> the blank expressionless stare of imbeciles:
> this is Toronto, not St. Petersburg on the Neva;
> though seas death and silent decades separate us
> we yet speak to each other, brother to brother;
> your forgotten martyrdom has taught me scorn
> for hassidic world-savers without guns and tanks:
> they are mankind's gold and ivory toilet bowls
> where brute or dictator relieves himself
> when reading their grave messages to posterity
> —let us be the rapturous eye of the hurricane
> flashing the Jew's will, his mocking contempt for slaves[15]

The other observation concerns his sense of a male-female dialectic that constantly demands his assertion of masculinity, a self threatened by images of castration or engulfment. Both are versions of a dialectic, sometimes cast in Nietzschian terms, sometimes simply as a mythicized version of the holy family of St. Urbain's street, that requires the poet to create himself daily. An apocalyptic-romantic version of ethnicity, then, Layton's story turns him, first, into the poet who dies, is reborn, dies, the self making itself over daily; and second, the monster, raging through suburbanite closets and bedrooms, the man from the ghetto remade, Duddy Kravits as poet-prophet:

> And if in August joiners and bricklayers
>   are thick as flies around us
> building expensive bungalows for those
> who do not need them, unless they release
>   me roaring from their moth-proofed cupboards
> their buyers will have no joy, no ease.
>
> I could extend their rooms for them without cost
>   and give them crazy sundials
> to tell the time with, but I have noticed
> how my irregular footprint horrifies them
>   evenings and Sunday afternoons:
> they spray for hours to erase its shadow.[16]

"Whatever else poetry is freedom," says Layton, yet "Mercifully it . . . is about poetry itself."[17] Self-realization, that is to say, like self-conscious-ness, is reflexive; it mirrors its own self or, as in the Freudian paradox about the artist, it finds real in fantasy what cannot be found in reality. "Though art transcends pain and tragedy," says Layton, "it does not negate them, does not make them disappear . . . poetry does not exorcise historical dynamism, macabre cruelty, guilt, perversity, and the pain of consciousness."[18] The distinction appears to me to be a vital one for this discussion. For what could be the nature of a transcendence that does not negate the reality it transcends? In the context of ethnicity or ethnic literature, the answer is, surely, the fictional or reflexive character of the subject itself.

If we now turn to a writer outside the Jewish tradition, we find the paradoxes of ethnicity repeating themselves the moment the subject is raised. Strictly, F.P. Grove's *A Search for America,* I suppose, is an American pastoral rather than an ethnic novel, but it properly belongs here since it takes its form first of all from an immigrant's experience and from the consequent question of identity, in this case, how to become an Ameri-can. The dialectic of *A Search for America* is a double one: Europe as opposed to America; the true America as opposed to the false one, both versions of what Warren Tallman calls the crude-fine paradox.[19] Grove brilliantly plays off these oppositions, resolving the Europe-America polarity by the further polarity of a true and false America which in turn he seeks to resolve in a final astonishing reversal that turns the true America into Canada. Of course, the search for America involves Grove in a search for himself, since it is his resolve to "cut himself loose from Europe" and to remake himself as a man in a new land. What is genuinely startling, absolutely explicit, and crucial to the argument of this paper in Grove's identification of himself is not only his identification of a true self with a fictional (or created) one, but the literal fact that for some 45 years historians and critics have taken the fictional autobiography to be an actual one. Who was Frederick Philip Grove? We now know, because of the brilliant scholarship of Douglas Spettigue, that what Grove told us in his Note to the Fourth Edition is to be taken seriously: his autobiography is fictional.[20] Grove is a fictional creation, twice removed from the actual in *A Search for America*.

Commenting on his own answer to the question whether the story presented in the book is fact or fiction, an answer which he says was "prevaricating," Grove adds:

> Imaginative literature is not primarily concerned with facts; it is concerned with truth. . . . The reason for this is that, in imaginative literature, no fact enters as mere fact; a fact as such can be perceived; but, to form subject-matter for art, it must contain its own interpretation; and a fact interpreted, and therefore made capable of being understood, becomes fiction.[21]

How traditional Grove's position here is may be suggested by considering the poetics of Browning, or James writing on the art of the novel, but for our purposes it is not tradition but the created self that matters. Grove tells us, after all, that the true self is fictional. He literally wrote himself into existence, created himself, wrote his own mythology, personal and social. The question as to why he so wrote may, in a literal sense, never be answered, though Spettigue seems now to have discovered evidence that disguise was necessary to Grove. Again, for our purpose, what is important is that the reason for fiction, the motivation of it, appears to be as much a literary as a biographical one. Grove hints at the power of duplicity as a source of creativity:

> The book which follows is essentially retrospective; which means that it is teleological; what was the present when it was written had already become its *telos*. Events that had followed were already casting their shadows backward. By writing the book, in that long ago past, I was freeing myself of the mental and emotional burden implied in the fact that I had once lived it and left it behind. But the present pervaded the past in every fibre.[22]

"He dramatized a personality," Frye says of Grove.[23] Precisely. But he left us then with the endless uncertainties and ambiguities implied by the need to dramatize and so create a self.

III

Two final questions remain: one concerning the generality of this notion of ethnic writing as a self-reflexive form; the other concerning language itself. By now, I expect, it would be obvious that I have taken a deliberately narrow and partial view of what constitutes ethnic writing, a literature existing at an interface of two cultures, a form concerned to define itself, its voice, in the dialectic of self and other and the duplicities of self-creation, transformation, and identities. By definition, that would seem to exclude at once as ethnic works those concerned with the life of a community or culture on its own terms. Whether this immediately excludes much of A.M. Klein's poetry, for example, "Portraits of a Minyan," say or "Baal Shem Tov," I'm not entirely certain, but I expect so. And while I might want to argue that Adele Wiseman's *The Sacrifice* and Klein's *The Second Scroll* could be shown to operate with the structures described here, especially since both are books about books in which questions of identity are uppermost, or that Jack Ludwig's *Confusions* belongs here for obvious reasons, I would feel less certain of a whole range of other works: Grove's prairie novels, for example, or Martha Ostenso's gothic romances; obviously, there is a sense in which the rendering of Jewish experience as in Klein, or Mennonite experience as in Rudy Wiebe's *Peace Shall Destroy Many,* or Scandinavian experience in Laura Salverson's novels, forms part of what normally we would describe as ethnic writing. But to repeat an argument I used in writing about John Marlyn's *Under the Ribs of Death* (a novel like Kriesel's *The Rich Man,* very much in the pattern I am concerned with here), it seems to me not only tasteless but futile to confuse questions of cultural identity with local colour. This is not a critical comment on any of the writers I mention, but on the uses of criticism itself. It seems to me an integrated community will not see itself in ethnic terms but as an authentic culture. Ethnicity presents itself as problem of self-definition. If, for example, we accept the B&B Commission version, we see at once how this is: "What counts most in our concept of an 'ethnic group' is not one's ethnic origin or even one's mother tongue, but one's sense of belonging to a group, and the group's collective will to exist."[24] This is perilously close to the definition put upon Griffin by Shalinsky, a definition that starts the whirligig going. Says Shalinsky, "A Jew is an idea. Today, you're my idea of a Jew."[25] A linguistic and cultural heritage is different from a definition. And it is on that ground of definition, and that alone, that I argue for the self-reflexive novel or poem of identities as ethnic.

It begins to appear here as if ethnicity might present itself as a problem only—or perhaps most acutely—in linguistic terms. We might say it is a problem of translation. My difficulty with this notion is my own lack of competence in languages, but it seems hardly necessary to insist on the cultural confusions involved in the translation process. Translating the poems of Akhmatova, Stanley Kunitz repeats the endless complaint: The poems exist in the integrity of their form and do not depend on imitable effects.[26] Accepting that perennial limitation, I was moved to think about ethnicity and language when I came across *Volvox:* an anthology of

"Poetry from the Unofficial Languages of Canada . . . in English Translation." Twenty-eight poets are represented and more than a dozen languages. As I read, it seemed to me I was not hearing or seeing what I had become accustomed to in English writing of the sort that has occupied me today. The poet's concerns, I thought, were not so much cultural as universal; as in Robert Zend's *Literary Criticism:*

> Liebnitz thought
> this is the best
> of all possible worlds
>
> Voltaire thought
> Liebnitz was wrong when he thought
> this is the best
> of all possible worlds
>
> Pirandello thought
> Voltaire was wrong when he thought
> Liebnitz was wrong when he thought
> this is the best
> of all possible worlds
>
> I think . . . but I'm wrong anyway.[27]

This can only be a guess and in any event it is qualified: but does the problem of ethnicity disappear in one's own language? Not always. Perhaps not with the Yiddish poets. Perhaps not with this writer obsessed with a lost home or that one for whom history is a record of dispossession. But at least once in *Volvox* the problem does appear and the writer tells us why. This is called *The Laundress* by Einar Pall Jonsson:

> She worked as a housemaid, then as a laundress
> in small town Winnipeg, full of emigres speaking
> every language except her own: she was Icelandic
> and as she worked she sang the old Icelandic hymns
> and songs: the songs had all her joy, they brought
> all her peace. She kept reaching for the language
> that got lost in her life. She could never speak it
> again, though it always measured her breath.
>
> Late one summer, as she lay dying, she sang again
> the Icelandic hymns, sang in her mother tongue,
> an other tongue for us; and as we lay her
> in a foreign grave, we, who know no Icelandic,
> who know then almost nothing of what she loved
> and lived by, say our prayers over her in English.[28]

In his recent collection of critical essays, George Steiner, who has been much occupied with questions of linguistics and culture, argues that there is a sense in which language, in its very structures of syntax and grammar, imposes cultural patterns and mythicizes the sense of self.[29] Could it be, then, that speaking another's tongue we cannot be ourselves, that the search for the lost self begins when we have been translated into another and will not end until there has been translation, transformation once again? The ending of John Marlyn's *Under the Ribs of Death* raises this cry, for a lost humanity, for a language free of deception, for a self that disappeared in a whirligig that begins with our "inescapable doubleness."

And yet another novelist, one who has reasons to know, insists on not the escape but the struggle. James Baldwin says

> From this void—ourselves—it is the function of society to protect us: but it is only this void, our unknown selves, demanding forever, a new act of creation, which can save us—"from the evil that is in the world." With the same motion at the same time, it is this toward which we endlessly struggle and from which, endlessly, we struggle to escape.[30]

NOTES

1. Elizabeth Janeway, *The New York Times Book Review*, October 21, 1973.

2. Margaret Atwood, "Afterword", *The Journals of Susanna Moodie* (Toronto: Oxford University Press, 1970), p. 62.

3. M.L. Lautt, "Sociology and the Canadian Plains", ed. Richard Allen, *A Region of the Mind*, Canadian Plains Studies Centre (Regina: University of Saskatchewan, 1973), p. 138.

4. R.D. Laing, *The Self and Others* (London: Tavistock Public, 1961), pp. 120-121.

5. Gloria Onley, "Power Politics in Bluebeard's Castle", ed. George Woodcock, *Poets and Critics* (Toronto: Oxford University Press, 1974), pp. 202-203.

6. Robert Kroetsch, "A Conversation with Margaret Laurence", ed. Robert Kroetsch, *Creation* (Toronto: New Press, 1970), p. 63.

7. George Woodcock, *Mordecai Richler* (Toronto: McClelland and Stewart Limited, 1970), pp. 23-24.

8. See Woodcock, p. 36.

9. Mordecai Richler, *The Apprenticeship of Duddy Kravitz* (New York: Paperback Library, 1964), pp. 249-250.

10. Woodcock, p. 52.

11. Rilke, "Archaic Torso of Apollo", but compare George Steiner, *In Bluebeard's Castle* (London: Faber and Faber, 1971), p. 41: *"We hate most those who hold out to us a goal . . . which, even though we have stretched our muscles to the utmost, we cannot reach. . . . "*

12. Edmund R. Leach, "Genesis as Myth", ed. Vernon W. Gras, *European Literary Theory and Practice* (New York: Dell Publishing Company, 1973), p. 320.

13. *Ibid.*

14. *Ibid.*, p. 318.

15. Irving Layton, *The Collected Poems of Irving Layton* (Toronto: McClelland and Stewart Limited, 1971), pp. 582-583.

16. *Ibid.*, p. 28.

17. Irving Layton, *Engagements* (Toronto: McClelland & Stewart, 1972), p. 84.

18. *Ibid.*, p. 85.

19. Warren Tallman, "Wolf in the Snow", ed. George Woodcock, *A Choice of Critics* (Toronto: Oxford University Press, 1966), p. 75.

20. Douglas O. Spettigue, *FPG The European Years* (Ottawa: Oberon Press, 1973).

21. Frederick Philip Grove, "Author's Note to the Fourth Edition", *A Search for America,* (Toronto: McClelland and Stewart, 1971).

22. *Ibid.*

23. Cited in Douglas O. Spettigue, *Frederick Philip Grove* (Toronto: Copp Clark Publishing Company, 1969), p. 1.

24. *The Cultural Contributions of the Other Ethnic Groups,* Vol. IV of Report of the Royal Commission on Bilingualism and Biculturalism (Ottawa: Queen's Printer, 1969), p. 7.

25. Mordecai Richler, *Cocksure* (Toronto: McClelland and Stewart, 1968), p. 245. Cited in Woodcock, p. 52.

26. *Poems of Akhmatova,* Selected, Translated and Edited by Stanley Kunitz with Max Hayward (Boston, Toronto: Little Brown and Company, 1973), p. 29.

27. Robert Zend, "Literary Criticism", *Volvox,* ed. J. Michael Yates (Port Clements: Sono Nisi Press, 1971), p. 134.

28. *Volvox*, p. 191.

29. Steiner, *In Bluebeard's Castle,* see esp. pp. 88-89.

30. James Baldwin, "Everybody's Protest Novel", *Notes of a Native Son* (New York, 1955), pp. 20-21.

Ecological Heroes
and
Visionary Politics

"The words of Amos could serve as the epigraph to this book. 'I hate, I despise your feast days, and I will not smell sacrificial offerings in your solemn assemblies.' "[1] The writer is Joseph Brodsky. His subject is Nadezdha Mandelstam's *Hope Abandoned*, the second volume of her celebrated memoirs of the poet, Osip Mandelstam, whose greatness we are only now coming to recognize. And as Brodsky's words suggest, there is a terrifying opposition within the memoirs between the poet and that which killed him, between, as Brodsky goes on to say, *culture* on the one hand and *society* on the other; between the intellect and authority, on the one hand, language and sex, on the other. It is a distinction with which this paper is primarily concerned. Mandelstam himself believed every poet writes his own death. What could that dark statement mean? What it meant to Solzhenitzyn, say, who spoke of poetry as a second government? Or what others have meant when they voiced suspicion that poetry may be not a catharsis, but a threat. In his study of suicide, *The Savage God*, Alvarez remarks how writers frequently find themselves confronted by a ferocious onrush of psychic material which they cannot handle.[2] And George Steiner, in his studies of contemporary culture, is led to consider whether poetry itself might not be the form of disorder.[3] Whatever differences there are among these writers—and it scarcely needs saying, the differences are profound—all confront precisely the same phenomena and the same question "how to live," as Brodsky says "without consolation," a question that posits "a moral degradation, devoid of national character and not determined by concrete political processes,"[4] a crisis in the values not only of civilization but of the humane arts themselves.

A certain order, a certain articulation, a certain patterning—these are taken to be attributes and vehicles of culture and civilization. It may be simple-minded to identify civilization with form, though the form-energy dichtomy is fundamentally what underlies Freud's analysis in *Civilization and Its Discontents,* and seems implied in Mill's essay on Bentham and Coleridge.[5] It is, nonetheless, clear that in criticism (whatever the larger social issues), the civilized tends to mean that which is formal and articulated, and the opposition "civilized—primitive" is frequently taken as "form-formlessness," primitivism involving the breaking apart of all form or a reversion to "earlier" or "distant" forms. Shortly, we shall see that these meanings can easily be turned about or confused, but initially, it remains, the primitive appears as satyr, id-figure, the archaic, in other words, a threat to an established order.

Consider this passage from Alvarez's study of suicide, *The Savage God:*

> Sixty odd years of genocide and intermittent war between super-powers which, like Freud's diseased super-ego, have become progressively harsher, more repressive and totalitarian, have made the modified ego-gratifications of civilization seem peculiarly fragile. The response of the arts has been to reduce the pleasure principle to its most archaic forms—manic, naked, beyond culture. The new strategy of aesthetic sophistication is primitivism: tribal rhythms on every radio, fertility rites on the stage, real or televised Gold Coast customs in the living-room, concrete poets grunting and oinking beyond language and beyond expression, *avant-garde* musicians exploring the possibilities of random noise, painters immortalizing industrial waste, radical politicians modelling their behaviour on the clowns of a Roman saturnalia, and a youth culture devoted to the gradual chronic suicide of drug addiction.[6]

Aside from all its other fascinating implications, I am interested in Alvarez's comment simply because its tone speaks so eloquently of the dread and horror he senses in a breakdown of order, even the order of literary forms. That is the point from which I want to begin. I want first to take the term "primitive" in two limited senses and only then consider what social or historical forces contemporary primitivism in Canadian poetry represents. It is always possible, of course, to take a poet on his own terms and to ask whether *his* analysis of his own society is serious enough to command out attention. We begin with his images, the forms and figures of his work.

One sense, then, in which I wish to use the word "primitive" is a formal sense. I mean by it a special version of literary form. A second sense in which I use the word is to refer to the symbolic use of the figure of primitive, that is, the appearance of Indians or Eskimos or native motifs (legends, for example) in a poem.

II

Wherever we place the beginning of modern poetry in Canada, it is clear enough that it has developed in something like an unbroken line to the present and that whereas in its earlier phases the question of *tradition* was a vexed one, the sense of a community of interest and integrity of purpose has grown. It might be more accurate to speak, as W.H. New does, not of a "community" but of "a major task," that of exploring "the landscape that is language itself, for the purpose of freeing the imagination from representational strictures and affirming the compatibility of spiritual (visionary) and political (empirical) goals."[7] It is exactly at this point, it seems to me, that is, when a sense of consolidation is replaced by a sense of experimental liberation, that the problem of primitivism, in some of its versions, appears.

As I have argued elsewhere, it is not difficult to discern in the poetry of Atwood, Newlove, Bowering, or Purdy the major tonalities of the contemporary writer's encounter with the land, space, with locality, with history, nor to see in that concerns defined in Canadian writing as early as E.J. Pratt's narrative poems and elaborated in the work of writers as various as Patrick Anderson, James Reaney and Jay Macpherson. Nor is it difficult to connect the sparseness and reticence of, say, Coleman or Bowering, with the imagism of Ross or with Souster's laconic style.[8] But to encounter the sound poems of B.P. Nichol, Joe Rosenblatt's *Bumblebee Dithyramb,* or the concretism of *The Cosmic Chef* is to enter a border country where the familiar terms of criticism no longer apply. The methods are by no means new. Their source, freely acknowledged by Nichol, his "Four Horsemen" and others, is the Dadaism of Hugo Ball and others. It is, I think, the *purpose* to which the new primitivism lends itself that is important.

Nichol's two volume *The Martyrology* (Coach House, 1972) may yet become the sacred book of contemporary primitivism in Canada, its cryptic phrases providing the necessary definitions and prayers, and a theory as well for all his earlier efforts:

the poem is written in spite of
all the words I once believed were saints.

But since *The Martyrology,* rather like *Canticle for Liebowitz,* or even Browning's *Death in the Desert,* poses large questions about perspective, language, history, and self-hood, I leave its clown-saint-word-magic language for the moment in favour of a writer who puts the question of form more immediately and sharply into focus, to return to Nichol in another context.

For some years now, at the rate of about six or eight per year, Bill Bissett has been producing mimeographed and stencilled books of poetry, or rather illuminated and occasionally engraved books. From those more or less underground Canadian presses, ganglia, very-stone house, blewointment press, talon, and weed/flower, the books pour out with their curious titles: "Where is Miss Florence riddle"; "we sleep inside each other all"; "The Gossamer Bed Pan"; "Sunday Work"; "liberating skies"; "lost angel mining company"; "what poeticks"; "S th story i to"; "blue trew"; "fires in the tempul"; "lebanon voices"; "of the land divine service"; "dragon fly"; "Awake in the Red Desert."

The last is a song-record book, a book accompanied by a record of Bissett chanting his poems along with a group of instrumentalists. Whether by accident or intention, there is no correspondence between the recorded and printed songs. Perhaps the fairest summary of Bissett's work, though he himself has no clear record of how much he has in fact written or where it is to be found, is contained in the Anansi selection made by Margaret Atwood and Dennis Lee, entitled *Nobody Owns th Earth* (Anansi, 1971). Characteristically, it contains emblem poems, concrete poems, incantatory poems, poems built on variations on one line or on two lines, songs, lyrics, allegories and Bissett's own drawings: mask-like faces with gleaming jewel-encrusted eyes; hairy suns; dancing figures linked, like paper cut-out people, in a row; flowers with faces inside of them. And, of course, the special spelling, grammar, language of the poems. This is the opening of "circles in the sun":

> In th mushroom village
> all th littul children
> brightly smiling
>
> in th mushroom village
> all th littul children
> brightly be
>
> asking only for th river
> asking only for th river

(Poets of Contemporary Canada, p. 113)

The sense in which we can speak of primitive formally refers first to the breaking apart of one version of literary form, the conventions of spelling, grammar, sentence, sentence structure. This is how Bissett puts it:

> the way is clear, the free hard path,
> no correct spelling, no grammar rules,
> you can live without the imperial sentence.

(Nobody Owns th Earth)

This is a preliminary, though by no means a trivial, step toward re-thinking the poem as spatial form. In Bissett's work as in Barry Nichol's, a new phonetics suggests the possibility of poetry as ideogram or pictograph, a re-arrangement of space and of our orientation toward it, so that visual and auditory responses intermingle. We might compare Rosenblatt's attempt to visualize (not imitate) the bee's flight and sound in his *Bumblebee Dithyramb* or perhaps the ultimate in concentrated visual—auditory punning, Nichol's line from *Still Water* (Talon Books, 1970)

> em ty.

At one level, the effort is to create *auditory space,* at another *visual sound,* both obviously totally different from the conceptual alphabet of the "literate" poem. Two parallels will suggest at once reasons for speaking of such poetry at "primitive"; one is the work of an eighteenth-century poet, Christopher Smart; the other the poetry (or sculpture) of contemporary Eskimo craftsmen. Smart's efforts in the *Jubilate Agno* (Harvard University Press, 1954) to work out new alphabets: of flowers (which he insisted had a language), of jewels, of letters, simply confirmed in the minds of many critics that he had been rightly confined to a madhouse. But a serious study of his comments on "voice" might suggest that at the very least Smart knew what he was up to:

> . . . the VOICE is from the body and the spirit—
> and is a body and a spirit.
> For the prayers of good men are therefore visible to
> second-sighted persons. (J.A. BI, 239-240)

Incongrous as it may seem, to put beside Smart's comments a contemporary anthropologist's remarks on the primitive sense of auditory space reveals surprisingly similar pre-occupations:

> The value we place on verticality (it influences even our perception) stems from the strength of literacy in our lives. Children must be taught it. Natives do not know it. And when the mentally ill in our society withdraw from the burdens of literate values, and return to non-vertical, non-lineal codifications, we call them child-like, and even note parallels with primitives. To lack of verticality can be added multiple perspective, visual puns, X-ray sculpture, absence of background, and correspondence between symbol and size: all examples of non-optical structuring of space.

> Auditory space has no favoured focus. It's a sphere without fixed boundaries, space made by the thing itself, not space containing the thing. It's not pictorial space, boxed in, but dynamic, always in flux, creating its own dimensions, moment by moment. It has no fixed boundaries; it's indifferent to background. The eye focuses, pinpoints, abstracts, locating each object in physical space, against a background; the ear, however, favours sound from any direction.[9]

Contemporary cultural anthropology and structuralism, of course, have been long engaged in a revaluation of primitivism, an effort that extends from the work of Cornford, Harrison, and Frazer through to Levi-Strauss. Reviewing Levi-Strauss, George Steiner remarks that what we call "primitive thought" may be related to "the world-picture of quantum mechanics and relativity. . . ."[10] This is a somewhat pretentious way of saying that the sense of time and space in so-called primitive art differs from that in literate cultures. Not surprisingly, the predominantly oral art of contemporary poetry presumes, not only in sound poetry but in its written forms, new space-time relationships. For just as visual space becomes auditory space, so time (the rhythm of the poem) is altered through the medium of hypnotic chant and fugal arrangement.

These are by no means original observations. But in the particular Canadian context, new possibilities do suggest themselves. If an altered rhythm or time offers the possibility of a vision quest and its illumination, it equally tears the writer away from his earlier sense of literate order. Magic or vision can be released only if causality (as opposed to synchronicity) and visual order can be destroyed: the *line* or *sentence*. Lately, Bissett has come to call this prison or order, America, and he equates it with the various kinds of imperialism that are, for him, America.

LOVE OF LIFE, th 49th PARALLELL   love of life, th 49th parallell
love of life, th 49th PARALLELL   love of life, th 49th parallell
love of life, th 49th parallell   love of life, th 49th parallell
love of life, th 49th parallell   love of life, th 49th parallell
love of life, th 49th parallell   LOVE OF LIFE, TH 49th PARALLELL

". . . in three days fish and guest spoil . . ."

dont yu see, in th seventies now

in th fifties they sent in their teachers, their poets, their pretty-eyed
    intellectuals who were kind, of far out, helpful, and looking for th
    academic freedom they cud find here, afraid from the dark bittr spell
    mccarthy had cast ovr ther land. we handid them jobs, places,
        freedoms, welcomd th guests, gave refuge

                                    then came ther business also
    ther monoplies, ther cars ther tv shows, now they have control so much of
our educational centres, th media, now there is no academic freedom
here now they have th place to control th minds of our children, ths
        guests

    now ther peopul arm themselves against us on th bordr between
our countries now if not for our strength and our independence of ther
fascist ways aftr th record industry nd rock show take ovr, rip off, aftr
ther draft dodgers, if not for our strength, our independence, wud cum

ther tanks, ther ballistik missiles, ther show of hate, ther army

    wrr not supposed to write just pretty verse describing only
the color
        or the sheen of th line of th pig trough th bosses
    them up there
    or them below th border
        try to bash our brains thru nor th spirit of th decoration,
        whats happening is going on now, sumthing is going on
in th changes, nor supposd to write just pretty verse, or how good it is,
how good yu feel sumtimes, how togethr yu are, how painlessly
    yu move yr spiritual elegance thru this veil of shit, that aint for
        poets.
        (*Nobody Owns th Earth,* pp. 65-66).

Canadian primitivism here envisages a kind of perceptual revolution, the resulting Canada being as much a state of mind as a place. The liberation of form and language implies some sort of social liberation, perhaps something like the Whole Earth Commune. This could be a visionary future (Margaret Atwood reads Bissett's position as individualist: "Paradise here and now is individual and sexual; Hell here and now is social and mechanical; but the potential for social redemption is present."[11]) But the possibility is also that, as in the image of natives, the liberating world is ancestral. We only begin to sense the full implications of the primitive when we see it not only as form but as symbol, the ancestral ghosts and demons of Canada, or at least of its poetry.

III

Margaret Atwood distinguishes between the appearance of native figures in American and Canadian literature, but there is one similarity: they are not presented as realistic figures but as psychological projections, the externalization of a fear or a desire; they are, that is to say, symbols. As symbolic form, the native figure is a projection "of something in the white Canadian psyche"; it is as well a mediating figure, "a potential source of magic, of a knowledge about the natural-supernatural world which the white man renounced when he became 'civilized' " and a possible "ancestor" whose legends and stories will reveal our true identity.[12]

As psychological symbol, primitive figures appear early in Canadian writing and recur with surprising frequency throughout. Atwood cites as versions of her victor/victim (fear/desire) pattern examples from *Brebeuf and His Brethern* to *People of the Deer* and *Beautiful Losers*. There's no need to multiply examples: by the time we have reached Cohen and, say, Ryga in his *The Ecstacy of Rita Joe*, we have seen virtually every variation on the sado-masochistic and social aggression theme played out, even to the point of the equating of Jew-Indian-Quebecois in a victim complex, the image for which is the long house as concentration camp or hospital for the insane. Richler's cannibalistic Eskimo-poet, Atuk, is the farcical version of the genuine savagery in a white community's technique of self-deception. It may be worth insisting that literary Indians and Eskimos are not outside of or external to white Canada but rather a definition of its own character.

Towards the end of Miss Atwood's discussion of the primitive figure, especially in its role of mediating figure and "ancestor," there is a hint of uneasiness: "It might well be argued that a knowledge of our origins is 'in truth' much more likely to require the exhumation of a pile of dead Scots Presbyterians and French Catholics. . . ."[13] This is an exceptionally difficult point. In part, it is once again the native as opposed to European opposition (America as against Europe, vulgar as against cultured, "West" as opposed to "East," colonial as opposed to nationalist, abstract design as opposed to social realism) that underlies so much in Canadian writing and history. In part, it raises the question of primitivism in a new and

109

important way. Perhaps the formulation of "psychological symbol" is inadequate to deal with the problem of ancestors and mediators. Another, less rigid, more suggestive formulation might be needed to account for the appearance and power of primitive figures, one that would link Indian and Eskimo with other contemporary versions of primitive power, killers, mad-woman, and schizophrenics, for example.

Commenting on "images" of Canada, Douglas LePan speaks of his fascination with masks:

> No one can tell yet what mask to carve for Canada, which type to choose—a pulp savage or a bank teller, a civil servant or a broke hustler or a signalman helping to keep the peace in Cyprus or the Gaza Strip— whether the face should be serene and adventurous, or withdrawn and introspective. No one can tell for certain yet whether Canada is one nation or two. The country reveals itself only slowly even to those who love it most, and much of its character still remains ambiguous.[14]

If one looks at LePan's poems, the comments acquire unusual resonance. Two of his poems, at least, end with a staring face: the "lust red manitou" of "Country Without Mythology," an ambiguous teetering figure, like the stone gods of Easter Island, forever commanding, forever silent; and in "Coureurs de bois" the image of "wild Hamlet with the features of Horatio," though this is held up against the earlier mask of LaSalle, the figure whose image haunts LePan. That demon of North America, as he suggests in his comments about masks, who tore the heart out of a continent.

As staring figure or mask, the primitive appears in Canadian writing as early as "The Onondaga Madonna" but its most evocative versions are LePan's and contemporary parallels like the masks of madness of Ondaatje's "sane assassin" or Atwood's Susanna Moodie, those and the jewel-eyed drawings of Bissett's books.

It may be that the peculiar fascination of the mask, for contemporary writers, is its doubleness. "The mask in a primitive festival," remarks Joseph Campbell, "is revered and experienced as a veritable apparition of the mythical being that it represents—even though everyone knows that a man made the mask and that a man is wearing it."[15] Those staring eyes are the eyes of a God, though the face behind the mask is of the poet we know. For the "civilized" poet like LePan, one suspects, the duplicity or ambiguity of the mask allows precisely the possibility he desires, at once an evocation of the primitive and yet not a surrender to it: double man, like the voyageur or like his own vision of a possible image of man, Canadian man as trapper and bourgeois; hence both Horatio and wild Hamlet. Layton's "primitives," Greek satyrs, too dream their dream of civilized forms, though his masks are not specifically native ones. And, of course, Purdy frequently organizes a poem on the contrast between himself and the ancient figures, ruins, or even manuscripts he contemplates. Something of the same doubleness (from another point of view "duplicity") informs Newlove's poem, "The Pride" but what distinguishes it is not simply that it seeks identities, identification with the primitive in image and story, but in the *poem* itself, attempting finally identification of mask and poet in what Miss Atwood calls "the amazing transformation of whites into Indians":

> a single line and
> then the sunlit brilliant image suddenly floods us
> with understanding, shocks our
> attentions, and all desire
> stops, stands alone;
>
> we stand alone,
> we are no longer lonely
> but have roots,
> and the rooted words
> recur in the mind, mirror, so that
> we dwell on nothing else, in nothing else. . . .
>
> *(Poets of Contemporary Canada,* p. 82)

Newlove's poem approaches the point of identifying the poem with the mask, in other words, seeing that the genuine primitivism which he seeks, so that he might have a memory and an identity, is not the past but the poem itself. The later stanzas seem to turn away from this, perhaps to a more complex, certainly a more qualified, linking of White and Indian.

It is at this point that concrete, sound poetry, the land tantras of Bissett, the bee songs of Rosenblatt, or the abstract fugal chants of Nichol separate from the "depiction" of the mask. They, so to speak, dance the mask itself. Whereas LePan holds up the mask for our contemplation, the sound poet weaves his own poem as a mask of god. It is as if, doing so, he will be transformed, becoming not simply an actor playing at—or even demonstrating—ways of saying "no" to an order he wishes to resist but a participant in a new way of being. His voice, then, will be one with all voices, universal. This, at least, seems to be the meaning of the great hymn-like movement of the opening passage of Bissett's "Nobody Owns th Earth." As the title suggests, it is an ecological hymn. The language of hallucination, of disorientation, of irrationality has here become the means of a political statement, a vision of a whole people moving toward a world that, unlike ours, will know nothing of national corporations, technology, guns, or even civil order:

> well they moved across th hill
> looming large ya cud say, th soft
> moon overhead will outwit us all,
> th old ones hooted, th babes grunting,
> well over th hill.

th women's arms, soft as th moon,
making circles, like th trees down
into th valley, how to move
a whole peopul.

we pray for our peopul, moving
together, to see this is how th Earth is,
Father, you let us walk on, live on,
teach us to grow together in Peace
on your Earth.

Seeing Father how th Earth is as
Women, giving, giving, and making
wound, flood of her sorrow, we do
not know enuff, and giving, giving

What is it, laughing how long th
sun rise, th hair of a whole peopul
sleeping under blankets, before fires, of
a whole peopul, on th hillside

a long dream, third eyes flowing
within th wheat fields, endless
as th eye is, th eye of the peopul reaches
out to a new gathering

cradled in th woman's arms, th
children stretch in th sun rays, for them
it is not a long dream, th world changed
as they slept, peed into Earth

(Nobody Owns th Earth, p. 80)

IV

To understand fully the contemporary poetry of primitivism and its
political implications may still be beyond the resources of criticism. And
certainly it is too soon to attempt to evaluate it on aesthetic grounds
alone, an attempt that would seem as incongrous as ill-judged. Its development in Canada may be seen as part of that continuing attempt by
Canadian writers to discover their own tradition, to seek out "roots," to
find "ancestors." No doubt, throughout the history of Canadian writing,
this attempt has turned the writer to strange by-ways. But the most
extreme and radical manifestations of the primitive, it now seems clear,
have less to do with history than with politics, less to do with the past
than the present. But even these terms are inadequate to the vision
implied in any struggle with language and with the values carried by
language. The poets business is with words. But also with poetry, freedom. W.H. New reminds us of Layton's claim "Whatever else, poetry is
freedom." He also reminds us that, as B.P. Nichol's *Martyrology* makes
clear, even language itself can imprison or distort, and that poetry finally
attempts both to articulate and transcend its articulation.[16] What politi-

cal order or social order or civilization, even were there one blessed place
for the poet, could contain that? B.P. Nichol writes

> is it the poem makes us dense?
> or simply writing, the act of ordering
> the other mind
> blinding us
> to the greater vision.[17]

NOTES

1. "Beyond Consolation", in *New York Review of Books*, XXI, No. 1 (Feb. 7, 1974), p. 14.

2. A. Alvarez, *The Savage God*, (London: Weidenfeld and Nicholson, 1971).

3. George Steiner, *Language and Silence* (New York: Atheneum, 1974).

4. *New York Review of Books*, p. 13.

5. *Mill on Bentham and Coleridge*, ed. F.R. Leavis, 1950.

6. A. Alvarez, p. 101.

7. W.H. New, *Articulating West* (Toronto: New Press, 1972), p. xxiv.

8. See "Introduction", *Poets of Contemporary Canada 1960-1970* (Toronto: McClelland and Stewart, 1972).

9. Edmund Carpenter, "The Eskimo and his Art" in *Canada: A Guide to the Peaceable Kingdom*, ed. William Kilbourn. (Toronto: Macmillan, 1972).

10. George Steiner, p. 244.

11. Margaret Atwood, *Survival* (Toronto: Anansi, 1972), p. 243.

12. *Ibid.*, pp. 91, 103.

13. *Ibid.*, p. 105.

14. Douglas LePan, "In Frock Coat and Moccasins", ed., William Kilbourn, *Canada: A Guide to the Peaceable Kingdom* (Toronto: Macmillan, 1972), p. 3.

15. Joseph Campbell, *The Masks of God: Primitive Mythology* (New York: The Viking Press, 1959), p. 21.

16. *Articulating West*, p. xxiii.

17. Cited in *Articulating West*, p. xxiii. The text is corrected. New reads "dance" for "dense."

The City
in
Canadian Poetry

"I don't know whether you know Mariposa. If not, it is of no consequence, for if you know Canada at all, you are probably well acquainted
with a dozen towns just like it."[1] The opening lines of Leacock's *Sunshine
Sketches* take us back to a world we think we once knew: elm-shaded
streets; Post Office, Fire Hall, and YMCA on the main intersection; two
banks, the hardware and general store, and "On all the side streets . . .
maple trees and broad sidewalks, trim gardens with upright calla lilies,
houses with verandahs, which are here and there being replaced by
residences with piazzas."[2] The "deep and unbroken peace"[3] of the small
town at the turn of the century before the great move to the city began,
before urbanization, before the megalopolis, before parkways and thru-
ways, before traffic and jackhammers and subways and noise:

> Can someone turn off the noise?
>
> The streets yearn for action nobler than traffic
> red lights want to be flags
> policemen want their arms frozen in loud movies:
> ask a man for the time
> your voice is ruined with static:
> >   What a racket! What strange dials!
> Only Civil War can fuse it shut—[4]

It seems obvious. It seems true. Once we were at "home" in the world,
in the definable, local place. Once we knew the little town with its square
streets and trim maple trees, almost within echo of the primeval forest.
Or did we dream it? "Mariposa," Leacock says, "is not a real town."[5] And
he goes on to suggest in the "Envoi" to *Sunshine Sketches* where he dreams
of how one returns to that other place, other time, that it exists only as a
version of a town that we in the cities *think* we remember. Mariposa is not
a place; it is a state of mind. It is the dream of innocence that we attach to
some place other than here and now.

In the burlesque mythology of *Sunshine Sketches,* Leacock plays on this dream of town and city: the city as an image of the small-town mind; the small-town as an image of the city-mind. And in so playing, he gives us a clue as to how in poem and story, town and city are metaphors. Some readers, of course, mistake them for real places. The particulars, the local colour, the details are there. Robert Creeley says, "locale is both a geographic term and an inner sense of being."[6] Raymond Souster gives us the feel, taste, smell, sense of the city of Toronto, its sensuous quality, though I, for one, have long felt his city some remembered place, a fantasy Torontonians particularly cherish of Yonge Street as a setting for a serious version of "Guys and Dolls." Souster is much more interesting as a poet concerned with the process of perception than as a poet of place.

To begin with Mariposa, then, is to begin at the beginning, the point where city and town intersect. Of course, historically, city and town exist before the turn of the century in Canada. Montreal glitters in half a dozen novels of the *ancien regime.* For Susanna Moodie, arriving in Canada in the 1830's, Quebec city appears as fortress, glorious crown of the citadel, and cholera-stricken charnel house. Halifax alternately thrives with a kind of animal vitality or sickens in a gloomy winter of poverty, following a rhythm that Haliburton's Sam Slick finds in its half-insect, half-human life. History does make demands upon poetry; places exist outside of the poem which describes them. But in poetry, place is metaphor, city is image, location is mythic. And so one begins, not with history, but with story; not with geography but with geographics—earth pictures, the line and model.

But what sort of model of a city could we find in a poem? James Reaney, who is a kind of Benjamin Franklin of Canadian poetry, sets out provisional answer in the "Second Letter" of *Twelve Letters to a Small Town* where he provides "Instructions: How to Make a Model of the Town":

First take two sticks and two leafy branches.
Put their ends together so they form spokes.
The spokes of an invisible wheel.
Coming together at the centre and fanning out—
These sticks and branches are
The principal through streets of the town.
Huron Street and Ontario Street can be leafy branch streets.
Downie and Erie can be the bare stick streets.

We'll make model houses out of berries.
Take some berries. Ripe gooseberries for red houses.
White raspberries for yellow brick houses. . . .
And trees can be represented by their leaves.
One elm leaf for a whole elm tree,
And streets laid out with rows of berry houses.
From the air, you know, a small town
Must look like rows of berries in the grass.

Now take some red apples and some russet apples,
Put these along the main streets for the business places.
Three potatoes each for the Court House
St. Joseph's Church (R.C.) and St. James's (C of E).
Buildings around the Market Square—ditto.

With a rather sharpside brick-coloured tomato in the centre
of the Market Square—to stand for the three towered
City Hall.[7]

Well, anyone who has been there will recognize Stratford, Ont., in Reaney's model of a town, I expect, though obviously no one will want to call the model realistic. But then why would Reaney want to build a model rather than attempt to show us the town itself in his poem? The answer seems to have something to do with things like totem poles and tribal clans, at least according to the anthropologist Claude Levi-Strauss. Writing about the complex ways in which totemic classifications work, Strauss is led to wonder whether "the small-scale model . . . may . . . in fact be the universal type of the work of art."[8] The peculiar pleasure we derive from models seems to be particularly related to their dimensions, Strauss notes, and he goes on to say that "In the case of miniatures, in contrast to what happens when we try to understand an object or living creature of real dimensions, knowledge of the whole precedes knowledge of the parts. And even if this is an illusion, the point of the procedure is to create or sustain the illusion, which gratifies the intelligence and gives rise to a sense of pleasure which can already be called aesthetic on these grounds alone."[9] From our own perspective, looking at the model, we see the whole of it at once: it is a universe, a universal, and we, as gods, play at creation, making and destroying cities, peoples, civilizations. Reaney's instructions on how to make a model town turn out to be instructions on how to write a poem.

But his poetic city or town holds a surprise. Its form is a natural form, since it is a town made out of objects of nature: leaf, branch, berry, fruit, food. At first glance, this is puzzling because we tend to think of the city as an unnatural rather than a natural form. Maybe Reaney wants us to think the city ought to be human rather than mechanical and so he uses images we associate with life, like images of nature, rather than images of artificial things, to suggest what a city is. Or should be. Or maybe, as a small town boy he simply associates the city in its best form with natural forms. Anyhow, in a poem called "Winnipeg Seen as a Body of Space and Time," part of a longer poem called "A Message to Winnipeg," Reaney contrasts two human bodies of Winnipeg, one made out of the objects of nature, the other made out of man's products. The natural body of Winnipeg Reaney obviously approves of, but the mechanical one horrifies him. The first is good because it humanizes nature or is a human nature; the second is bad because it turns man into a machine, or at least mechanizes a city. The good city is a projection of life into nature; the bad one projects a mechanism into life.

As good city of the past, Winnipeg had the shape of a human body with arms of burr oaks and ash-leaf maples; its backbone a crooked silver muddy river; its thoughts ravens in flocks; its bones, snow. As bad city of the present, its shape can be described best as collapsed mechanical:

> A boneyard wrecked auto gent, his hair
> Made of rusted car door handles, his fingernails
> Of red Snowflake Pastry signs, his belly
> Of buildings downtown, his arms of sewers,
> His nerves electric wires, his mouth a telephone,
> His backbone—a cracked cement street.[10]

I suppose there is some history in all this about the development of a natural site into a machine for living, and Reaney's poem does seem to work with the familiar contrasts of city and country, innocence and experience, naivity and sophistication, the organic and the mechanical. So it becomes possible to think that cities like Winnipeg once were organic, vital human places to live but now have collapsed into boneyards of used cars, the cemetry of the mechanical, a brittle, littered inhuman junkyard, "crawling with the human fleas/Of a so-so civilization—half gadget, half flesh."[11] But if Reaney means this to be any kind of fact about Winnipeg, obviously he hasn't read Frederick Philip Grove, let alone any sociologists.

Actually, Reaney's "boneyard Winnipeg" suggests something more than a fall from pastoral innocence and simplicity as the explanation of contemporary ills. The collapsed or broken giant recalls figures in Blake and the Bible and it is these Reaney wants us to remember rather than any simple-minded theory about 19th century spontaneity in the small town and 20th century wickedness at the corner of Portage and Main. To see what he wants to evoke, we can look at another version of the same image. It is one which appears in Canadian poetry as early as Lampman's *City of the End of Things,* a poem of astonishing power and an eerie kind of prophetic force. In Lampman's vision of an automated city, an unholy trio rules, while a fourth, more hideous, figure guards the city's gates. Within its walls, the city burns with a thousand furnaces, and somewhere there sounds incessantly an inhuman music. These motifs—the blazing furnace, the three who walk there accompanied by a shadowy fourth, the city built to music—belong to the magic cities of legend and poem: Troy and Camelot, and the fiery furnace of the Bible where three walked unharmed protected by the angel of god. But just as Pandemonium, Milton's version of Hell, is a parody or upside-down version of the city of God, so Lampman's city parodies divine and magic places. Ultimately, it takes a single shape—or rather everything else falls away to reveal one shape alone:

One thing alone the hand of Time shall spare
For the grim Idiot at the gate
Is deathless and eternal there.[13]

I doubt that Lampman intends to frighten us with stories of mechanical monsters. The poem, by means of parody, evokes the horror of a *mindless* world. In other words, Lampman sees the real opposition not between the nature and machine, but between nature and imagination. The machine he is writing about is nature itself.

The model we started with has now changed shape several times: it has been leaf, twig, fruit, berry; boneyard auto gent; mechanical man; fiery furnace; fallen giant—and in the process of changing shape it seems to have changed position too, not only geographically, from Stratford to Winnipeg, but mentally, from the image of city as technological horror to the image of nature itself as a machine. Now, the problem before the poet is twofold: first, whether it is possible to put together the world and the model, nature and imagination; and second, if it is not possible, how to get past nature itself. For both parts of the question the city seems to be a crucial image.

For example, the effort to put the world and the model together is made in one of the most eloquent poems we possess, A.M. Klein's *Autobiographical,* the crucial setting for which is the city of Montreal.

We live always in duplicity, in a double world of memory and fantasy, time and imagination, event and dream. And it is out of this duplicity that Klein weaves a double image of Montreal. Like the double-exposure in a photograph, the image places one pattern over another, one being occupying two spaces at the same time. Perhaps one could have expected to find paradoxical pictures of Montreal simply because of its complicated French-English-Jewish ethos; or it may be that the paradoxes emerge only from Klein's own Talmudic and legalistic mind, his vivid memories, his extraordinary awareness of the tradition in which he writes, at once Hebraic, English, literary, and visionary, domestic and fabulous. No matter, Klein's Montreal is, on the one hand, a memory of his boyhood; on the other, a fabled city of Jewish lore, imagination, and scripture. Interweaving Oriental, Yiddish, European, and local images, the poem transforms and transmutes all that it touches: ghettoes become pleasant bible land; the candy store, a treasure cave of spices and jewels; and yet everything remains as it was, living again in memory. Concentrating on childhood remembrance, Klein recalls Wordsworth's approach to poetry, but only to reject the Wordsworthian notion of poetry as tranquil recollection; and where Wordsworth equated childhood with nature, Klein equates it with the city of his boyhood. That city recalls another poet's effort to disengage from nature a timeless moment. It is like Yeats's Byzantium, like the sacred palaces of romantic poetry, like the goal of the messianic quest; and yet in recalling Yeats, the poem rejects him. Where Yeats seeks to be gathered into the artifice of eternity and to burn away the mortal body, Klein turns to his own youth there to find the fabled city. Where Yeats turns away from youth to age, the "sages standing in God's holy fire," the "Monuments of unaging intellect,"[14] Klein turns away from age to youth,

> . . . the first flowering of the senses five,
> Discovering birds, or textures, or a star,
> Or tastes sweet, sour, acid, those that cloy;
> And perfumes.[15]

And where Byzantium stands outside of nature, Klein's Montreal exists both in and out of time: as memory, in time; and as fable, out of time, poised somewhere between the world of eternal forms and the world of transient human memory, between pure image and event. The magical city of boyhood thus becomes the possibility of God's city promised in scripture: the jargoning city (Babel, perhaps) becomes the fabled city (the New Jerusalem). Therefore, the past validates the future. History moves to the fulfillment of God's purposes. The fabled city of the past, of memory and scripture, was once and will be again, and the poet can write:

> I am no old man fatuously intent
> On memories, but in memory I seek
> The strength and vividness of nonage days,
> Not tranquil recollection of event.
> It is a fabled city that I seek;
> It stands in Space's vapours and Time's haze.[16]

Montreal, of course, shows up as setting and symbol in a host of novels and poems. There is Richler's Montreal, and Cohen's Montreal, MacLennan's, Layton's, Gabrielle Roy's, Dudek's, Scott Symon's. But whatever the reason, it seldom appears as the magical city it is in Klein's poem. In fact, few cities in Canada tempt the poet with imagery of the fabulous or magical. And a surprising number are seen in flames or as cities of the dead or as doomsday towns. Reaney's *Message to Winnipeg* concludes with a horrendous warning of dreadful things about to happen to Child's and Eaton's and Hudson's Bay. In a splendid and justly praised poem, Wilfred Watson sees Calgary as Golgotha, and as the valley of dry bones where clothes flapping on clotheslines are ghastly reminscences of crucifixions and of Ezekiel's prophecy that these dry bones shall live:

> . . . In the cemetery of the sun below
> All the houses of the living were tombs;
> And I saw Calgary a hill of tombstones
> Rising under a coast of mountains
> Washed in the cold of my sun of cloud.
> When I walked to the wither of my day
> In this city where every backyard had
> Its cross and clothesline white and sere

With sereclothes shining in the sun
Of my first despair of resurrection

Came my first Monday of darkness. It
Was the week's hanging and drying noon.
All the drought of my bones was for water.
And the ghosts of my people flapped about
Me in this washday blow and weather.[17]

Through the poet's visionary eyes, his improved binoculars, as Layton calls them, the whole city takes fire. Montreal explodes, prophetically enough we might now say, at the corner of Peele and St. Catherine, and the poet, looking down on the holocaust, takes oddly detached notice of the behaviour of citizens in that fire. Is it by the way to observe that the most sustained and finely articulated piece of prose description in the Canadian novel is Hugh MacLennan's account of the Halifax explosion in 1917? Winnipeg, Calgary, Montreal, Halifax, a fair enough list, one supposes. Of course, from another perspective the fires of the city can be seen as something quite different from a natural holocaust or a doomsday vision. Earle Birney, to judge from his verse play *The Trial of a City* or *The Damnation of Vancouver,* has no great love to spare for that coastal place, and indeed by the end of the play the suggestion seems fairly clear that doomsday is at hand for Vancouver too. But looking down at the city from the mountains around, in "Vancouver Lights" he sees it as a Promethean defiance of darkness, as the spark of human creativity, and as a mirror or model of the universe itself, a human galaxy answering or corresponding to the galaxies of light in the great darkness of the heavens and amid the great dark of the earth itself.

The fire that burns in so many poems on Canadian cities now may be seen to be the fire of the poet's own creativity burning away the dead husk of the city or the machinery of the natural world. The answer to the question "how to get past nature?" is: by means of imagination. The furnace or forge symbolizes creative energy, and in that forge new images are hammered into being. The flames of the burning city turn out to be the golden or jewelled pavement of the redeemed city. These are the flames that we see in the golden smithies of the emperor in Yeats's "Byzantium," to take a famous example:

At midnight on the Emperor's pavement flit
Flames that no faggot feeds, nor steel has lit,
Nor storm disturbs, flames begotten of flame. . . .

Those images that yet
Fresh images beget. . . .[18]

In that same fiery furnace of imagination, Layton's Montreal is transformed. After the explosion at Peele and St. Catherine, where "under the green neon sign" the poet sees only "ruined corpses of corpulent singers,"[19] in a skeletal world of teeth and crosses, he seeks new eyes and another tree to supplant the fiery cross that inflames his city. Through the long night the fires burn until a new world emerges:

> All night, all night the autos whizzed past me
> into heaven, till I met men going there
>   with golden nails and ravens whose wings
> brushed the night up the tall sides of buildings
> and behind them in the morninglight the windows shone
> like saints pleased with the genius that had painted them.[20]

Cosmological transformations, like those we have been observing here, occur in the Bible where, for example, the jewels of Aaron's breastplate form at one and the same time the pattern of the jewelled temple of Solomon, the tribal symbols, the blazing walls of the New Jerusalem, and the constellations of the Zodiac. It is tempting to think there may be a simple geographical explanation for Canadian poets' finding the pattern an appropriate one. One thinks, for example, of the perspective of Canadian cities seen from the air at night, jewels and stars strung out along a necklace of highways. Our cities enlarge or diminish remarkably as we leap toward or away from them at jet speed, and the contracting and expanding suggests at once the possibilities of total transformation. More than anything else, of course, the cities exist amid vast spaces, fortresses or garrisons in a wilderness, island universes in a sea of darkness, models of the universe itself. The transcanada flight seems irresistibly to suggest cosmic dimensions, as in Earle Birney's early version of it in the old days of the North Star flights where prairie highways appear below the plane "dim and miraculous as Martian lines"[21] and Toronto is a galaxy. In F.R. Scott's "Trans Canada", the plane leaps away from Regina which falls below it like a pile of bones, and the poet meditates on the mystery and loneliness of space:

> I have sat by night beside a cold lake
> And touched things smoother than moonlight on still water,
> But the moon on this cloud sea is not human,
> And here is no shore, no intimacy,
> Only the start of space, the road to suns.[22]

Scott's cross-country flight returns us from the creative forge of imagination to actuality, to space. A curious fact about Canadian writing is the double presence in it of ancient time and vast space. The one, time, appears as the folding into the present of the past: biblical or primitive or mythic or childhood time. The other, space, appears as the wilderness of the ocean. Even in Vancouver, near falsemouth creek, Birney walks brooding like a wanderer in an Anglo-Saxon poem about the eternal tides of time and darkness around him. Our space is the emptiness between the cities and the stars, or even the emptiness in the modern city itself. If Montreal burns in the fires of time and poetry, Toronto is a void, an abyss. At least, it shows itself as the void to one of our most civilized poets, Dennis Lee.

Lee's remarkable *Civil Elegies* is a book of seven brooding meditations on civility, civitas, the possibility of life in the modern city. Lee's symbol for the city is the civic square: an emptiness at the heart of the city, a form of space, a place to which people come:

> The light rides easy on people dozing at noon in Toronto, or
> here it does, in the square, with white jets hanging
> upward in plumes on the face of the pool and the
> Archer composing the distance, articulating
> pockets and whorls, in what heroic space?—
>
> Nothing is important.
>
> But if some man by the pool . . .
> > if that man comes upon the void
> > > he will
> go under, or he
> must himself become void.[23]

Like the hero of Cohen's *Beautiful Losers* who is most present at the point where he is most absent from himself, Lee finally conceives of absence as the creative point where anything is possible, all possibilities exist. And the city exists in its emptiness, giving us "access to new nouns: as, tree, lintel, tower, body, cup."[24] A city and a country that are nothing, "asymmetric pin points dotted at random/through tracts of emptiness"[25] may be everything, says Lee:

> . . . and I learned to dwell among absence in jubilee,/declaring that all things which release us, all things which speed us into/calamity, as Canada, are blessed.[26]

So space, place, city come to be defined:

> an open place   a square or market place
> extension in two (or three) directions
> a part of the earth
> > earth picture
> place of battle field
> city town village hamlet dwelling house
> seat mansion manor-house country-house
> fortress   or a strong place
> a place of amusement
> the apparent position of a heavenly body on the celestial sphere
> "Who would kiss the place to make it well?"
> "A falcon towering in her pride of place"
> a proper appropriate or natural place
> a fitting time   a room reasonable ground

NOTES

1. Stephen Leacock, *Sunshine Sketches of a Small Town* (Toronto: NCL, 1960), p. 1

2. *Ibid.,* p. 2.

3. *Ibid.,* p. 2.

4. L. Cohen, *Flowers For Hitler* (Toronto: McClelland & Stewart, 1968), p. 35.

5. Leacock, p. xvi.

6. Robert Creeley, *A Quick Graph.*

7. James Reaney, *Poems* (Toronto: New Press, 1972), p. 212-213. This presents a condensed version of a portion of Reaney's poem, itself actually in the form of a dialogue.

8. Claude Levi-Strauss, *The Savage Mind* (University of Chicago Press, 1966), p. 23.

9. *Ibid.,* pp. 23-24.

10. Reaney, p. 133.

11. *Ibid.,* p. 133.

12. *Ibid.,* p. 133.

13. Archibald Lampman, *Lyrics of Earth* (Toronto: Musson, 1925), p. 263.

14. W.B. Yeats, *Selected Poems & Two Plays* (Collier Books, 1962), p. 95.

15. A.M. Klein, "Autobiographical", from *Collected Poems* (Toronto: McGraw Hill, 1974), p. 273.

16. *Ibid.,* p. 273.

17. Wilfred Watson, "In The Cemetery of the Sun", *Friday's Child* (London: Faber & Faber, 1955), pp. 34-35.

18. Yeats, pp. 132-133.

19. Irving Layton, "Winter Fantasy", *Collected Poems of . . .* (Toronto: McClelland and Stewart, 1971), p. 162.

20. *Ibid.,* p. 163.

21. Earle Birney, "North Star West", *Collected Poems of . . .*: Vol. I (Toronto: McClelland & Stewart, 1975), p. 157.

22. F.R. Scott, "Trans Canada", *Selected Poems* (Toronto: Oxford University Press, 1966), p. 35.

23. Dennis Lee, "Second Elegy", *Civil Elegies* (Toronto: Anansi, 1968).

24. *Ibid.,* "Seventh Elegy".

25. *Ibid.*

26. *Ibid.*

Cohen's Life
as a
Slave

It is probably necessary to apologize for attempting a serious discussion of Leonard Cohen's poetry, so quickly do contemporary "media Creations", as one of our critics insists on describing Cohen, become debased coinage. Of course, his work does present actual problems. I remember once a high-minded Canadian poet taking me to task because I chose to treat a cartoon poem of B.P. Nichol's with high-minded critical seriousness. The subject, I was told, was beneath me. And, another Canadian writer once muttered to me darkly after seeing a performance of Michael Ondaatje's *Collected Works of Billy the Kid*, "All that beautiful language wasted on a character who is so unsavoury." Certainly serious criticism of a writer like Cohen suffers from the difficulty that he refuses to take his work seriously: the victory of style over vision apparently undercuts any attempt to elucidate his subject or to examine his themes. But the effort, it seems to me, is worthwhile not simply because, in his development as a writer, he represents contemporary sensibility, but because his treatment of what, for want of a better term, could be said to be the writer's problem, the difficulty of being a writer, remains one of the most scrupulous and uncompromising we possess. To speak of Cohen in these terms, as a representative and uncompromised writer, I realize will sound peculiar, the more so if one looks at a collection of poems like *The Energy of Slaves,* his latest book, apparently as shoddy a piece of work as one would find anywhere today.

Of course, it is precisely this question of shoddiness that concerns me in this paper. Most contemporary writing presents itself in ways that to a traditional critic of literature, or to one concerned with the central place of literature in a humanist tradition, will seem problematical. George Steiner, for one, devotes much of *Language and Silence* to the paradoxical situation that it is the best of the humanist tradition—humane knowledge, literacy, and civilizing intelligence—that has been put to the worst uses. And he remarks as well on the shoddiness of contemporary imagination, its attraction to dark and rubbish-strewn corners of human experience, its obsession with the irrational, the brutal, the inhumane. Consider, he says, the contemporary writer's concerns: the exalting of the criminal as saint in Genet's plays and novels; the brutish mockery in Wm. Burroughs' mechanical manipulation of character; those human beings shoved into the ashcans of Beckett's drama; the saintly garbage heap of Ginsberg's America; the "mawkish sadism"—it is Steiner's term—of Tenessee Williams; or again to put it as he does, the "absurdly diminished and enervating view of human existence" implied by Salinger's "rococo virtuosity"[2]; we can add to the list: the elegant hollowness of John Barth's imitation of Borges; the shabby theatricality of Norman Mailer; the furtive pornography of Robert Lowell; poetry itself turned into featureless sound clusters, the ragged hallucinogenic mutterings and yowls of Michael McLure's tantras; or at best, the manic perceptions of Sylvia Plath in the terrible radiance that preceded her suicide; the syntactical contortions of John Berryman's *Dream Songs* rehearsing his own tortured leap to death. The list is random, but I hope typical. For it points to the dilemma of a criticism confronted with intractable material, what Northrop Frye refers to as "reactionary and anti-social attitudes,"[3] "quite obviously silly, perverse, or wrong-headed,"[4] and what others, notably Charles Olson, Warren Tallman, and Susan Sontag, have seen as a profoundly anti-humanistic impulse, a deliberate rejection of the myths, metaphors, and values of humanism.

There is a tendency now to speak of contemporary concerns with incompleteness, irresolution, fabrication as "post-modern", presumably with the implication that sometime about 1946—no one will be precise about old-fashioned matters of chronology—the consciousness of Western man suffered a sea-change. That is to say, one definition of a very vexed development is to see it simply as anti-modern, an opposition to its immediate ancestors.[5] Recently Harold Bloom has created a minor sensation with his argument that great writing, writing of magnitude, consists of re-writing the past: sons turning themselves into fathers, Blake re-writing Milton, Eliot attempting to show that all previous English literature imitated him, criticism as misreading. But the contemporary impulse, to borrow a phrase from Robert Kroetsch, is rather to erase, unwrite, un-invent the past, to write as if literature did not exist or had never existed, to create (if such a paradox is possible) an anti-art. And so while it is not my purpose to rehearse cultural history, I take it the cultural context to which Cohen's work responds is the one formulated as early as 1960 in Harry Levin's remarkable paper *What was Modern?* and recently taking on its Canadian shape in works as diverse as Frank Davey's *From There to Here,* Warren Tallman's "The Wonder-Merchants" and Kroetsch's own comments in *Boundary/2.* Kroetsch's words perhaps can serve as a summary: "He writes then, the Canadian poet . . . knowing that to fail is to fail; to succeed is to fail."[6] If this sounds like the Victor/

Victim formula made familiar by Atwood's *Survival,* it should surprise no one, though in detail, in the texture and drama of Cohen's poetry, it proves to be something different and I think more demanding.

The point of departure for this paper then is Leonard Cohen's *The Energy of Slaves,* and while the questions it raises are those by-now-familiar ones of "post modern" theorizing, I think the extreme version given to them by Cohen's new poetry makes it worth going over the same territory once again. My argument is simply that *The Energy of Slaves* belongs in the context not only of Cohen's earlier work, from which it does not represent any radical departure, but also in the context of Cohen's reading of the contemporary writer's difficulties with art and language. I take *The Energy of Slaves* to be another variation of Cohen's continuing concern with the meaning of *transformation* or (in an older language) transcendence, its necessity for the writer, his inevitable failure. If we take the term "myth" in Sartre's sense—a naming ceremony repeating or re-enacting a personal drama—the mythic moment of Cohen's work appears to have something to do with bodily transformation, the metamorphosis of Ray Charles at the end of *Beautiful Losers,* for example, or the equally remarkable changes in the speaker of "The Cuckold's Song":

> The fact is I'm turning to gold, turning to gold
> It's a long process, they say,
> it happens in stages.
> This is to inform you that I've already turned to clay.[7]

The mode of address too is important. Cohen's lyrics of transformation vary from formally-structured songs addressed to a traditional lover/mistress, as in "Dead Song", to versions of the dramatic monologue, "The Cuckold's Song" I suppose could serve as an example, through a variety of dramatic addresses in which the "you" spoken to becomes more or less explicitly the reader or audience. As in Margaret Atwood's "You are Happy", Cohen's later work, beginning with *Flowers for Hitler* and his songs, develops a murderously ambiguous seduction/repulsion pattern pointing, I think, to a troubled, difficult sense in his poetry of two conflicting demands, the demands of audience, the demands of art. The "you" of the poems, beckoning/beckoned, helps to work out a cultural dialectic of surprising complexity and consistency, stages in the process of transformation. Here, I trace out in a crudely schematic way some major patterns of Cohen's work that help to account for this dialectic and explain the meaning of transformation.

Three terms that can be used for convenience are "context", "persona", and "object", roughly corresponding to "field", "mode", and "tenor" in linguistics, or in less barbaric language, I suppose, "subject", "speaker", and "intention." The context for Cohen's first book, *Let Us Compare Mythologies,* is art; the persona, the artist; the object, vision or martyrdom. For his second book, *A Spice Box of Earth*, the context is love; the persona, the lover; the object, purification or priesthood; with *Flowers for Hitler*, the songs, and to an extent *Beautiful Losers*, the context becomes history; the persona, the junkie; the object expiation. This is an admittedly awkward way of pointing to a development in which Cohen's highly literary and academic early poems are succeeded by his love lyrics, among them eight or ten of the finest poems in the language, which in turn give way to ironic fantasies that presage the bitter attack on both audience and art in *The Energy of Slaves*. Abstracted from his ceremoniousness and rhetoric of ritual and lacking his imagery of hanged gods, mutilated lovers, angels, corpses, and demented saints, this scheme does less than justice to his work, but it throws a sharp light on a major design in his writing: the tension between art conceived of as a dream of perfection, a transforming power, and history experienced as a nightmare of monstrous proportions and imperfection. The subtle decadence of Cohen's earlier poems in which a dream of high art is flavoured with spicy hints of torture turns into the melodrama of the later poems in which a history of horror is flavoured with the spice of sexual fantasies. This is to say no more than that Cohen's work is a series of variations on a theme of sado-masochism, but at the same time to recognize the deepening nature of his vision in which the later poems pose—through image and manner—a disturbing question about the involvement of art and private fantasy in a public nightmare of dreadful dimensions. Yet the answer apparently attempted by Cohen—a radical critique of humanism—turns into a parody of itself, grotesque manoeuvering in the labyrinths of personality, melodramatic posturing, the poet as Nazi or Junkie, main-liner instead of traditionalist. In brief, the question put by his poetry concerns the meaning of the poet's involvement in mass art and popular culture.

It is worth remembering, Cohen literally experienced the betrayals forced upon him by the mass audience he sought and found, particularly the betrayal involved in identifying a remote, timeless visionary world with the vulgar fantasies of popular culture. His characteristically mocking blend of stylized phrasing and pop imagery seems designed at once to exploit and make light of this identification that clearly excites and disturbs him.

Like the earlier *Flowers for Hitler*, much of *Beautiful Losers* is devoted to exploring these secret links between art and mass culture. In fact, Cohen's manipulation of the new possibilities released by his paralleling of high with low culture accounts, I believe, in part for both the brilliance and popularity of *Beautiful Losers* which, on the face of it, ought to have been a staggering failure on the market because of its obscurity, complexity, and erudition. Yet its pyrotechics of style and language, far from repelling an audience supposedly on the verge of illiteracy, brought new worshippers at the feet of still another guru of the sixties media. Still, to explain Cohen's success solely in sociological terms, it seems to me, is an exercise of monumental futility and vulgarity and (if it were not a contradiction in terms to say so) transient interest. More important than its popular success is the stylistic discovery Cohen exploited in his writing. I suspect that the extraordinary energy flowing through the book originates in Cohen's sudden understanding of the real driving power of his imagination. That dynamo proved, after all, not to be the literature and tradition hallowed in the English Department of McGill, and honoured in Cohen's revealing title of his first book *Let Us Compare Mythologies,* but the popular culture on which he had been raised and the personal fantasies which not only fed upon the fascist masters with a comic book mythos but sprang from his own obsessions. In 1962 at a conference of writers in Foster, Quebec, a gathering of a strange group called "English Writers of Quebec," Cohen, who had just won a CBC prize for a ms of poems entitled *Opium for Hitler,* an early version of the later *Flowers for Hitler,* announced his new literary programme. Henceforward, he told a startled group that included such imposing figures as the controversial poet Irving Layton, the critic Milton Wilson, the shy pornographer of the Eastern townships John Glassco, and a horde of shadowy luminaries—poets and literati—he would seek his audience in *Playboy* and *Esquire,* not in little magazines in which poets write for other poets. His instinct, I believe, was poetically right, not commercially motivated. He had grasped what remains surely one of the major directions of contemporary or post-modern writing, its determined anti-literary, anti-humanist impulse.

To put the issue between modern and contemporary as one between the literary and anti-literary in writing—or between elitist and mass culture—I realize will sound extraordinarily simple-minded. Yet the point is worth considering. The mythology of Olson's *Maximus* poems, after all, is personal, local and historical rather than literary, general, and timeless; W.C. Williams chooses to mythologize not Troy but Paterson, New Jersey; a procedure distinct from Pound's poetic archeology in the *Cantos* that give us a multi-layered hero, a Ulysses who has seen many cities, many men, who speaks not only the lingo of Williams' persona but the rhetoric of epic, romance, and lyrics. It is true, of course, that the same tension between a mythopoeic European culture and an experiential American one—between the fine and the crude as Warren Tallman would have it—underlies Walt Whitman's ironic demythologizing of literature and is explicitly recognized in Pound's line "I make a pact with you, Walt Whitman." It is also true that Northrop Frye's brilliant point about the technique of displacement enables us to understand that the real distinction is not between realism and mythologizing. Twain's river story repeats a story as old as that in Williams' *Paterson* and Olsons' *Maximus;* the quest pattern of the one, and the city who is a giant man in the other two works, are as old as the Bible, if not older. But what

128

structural principles tell us about is form, and though it is customary now to make light of content, the *interest* of the writer in the details of a felt life, as Henry James would put it, to abandon the habits of allusion, the manner of speech, the rhetoric, the profound familiarity of a whole culture, a way of being, could prove to be more significant than in our more rigorously aesthetic moments we might believe.

In short, to turn to Canadian examples, when Margaret Atwood chooses the photograph in place of the reduplicating images of the Persephone story, when Gwen MacEwen turns to magicians and pea-nut-butter sandwiches rather than the oft-told stories of Athens and Jerusalem, when Michael Ondaatje finds his text in forgeries of the legend of *Billy the Kid* and the methodology of spaghetti westerns, we can suspect not only that new literary techniques are being employed but that new sensibilities are demanding their own inventions. Robert Kroetsch speaks not only of uninventing the world but the two prior acts of imagination in what he takes to be a development of a post-modern sensibility: the first, naming, inventing the world; and second, re-naming or re-inventing it. The first great cataloguing of words, something like A.M. Klein's Adamic poetic activity, we recognize as a traditional version of poetic power of the sort modernists claimed for themselves.

> . . . Look, he is
> the nth Adam taking a green inventory
> in world but scarcely uttered, naming, praising,
> the flowering fiats in the meadow, the
> syllabled fur, stars aspirate, the pollen
> whose sweet collusion sounds eternally.
> For to praise
>
> the world—he, solitary man—is breath
> to him. Until it has been praised, that part
> has not been. Item by exciting item—
> air to his lungs, and pressured blood to his heart—
> they are pulsated, and breathed, until they map,
> not the world's, but his own body's chart!
>
> And now in imagination he has climbed
> another planet, the better to look
> with single camera view upon this earth—
> its total scope, and each afflated tick,
> its talk, its trick, its tracklessness—and this,
> this, he would like to write down in a book!
>
> To find a new function for the déclassé craft
> archaic like the fletcher's; to make a new thing;
> to say the word that will become sixth sense;
> perhaps by necessity and indirection bring
> new forms to life, anonymously, new creeds—
> O, some how pay back the daily larcenies of the lung![8]

The second prior act of imagination seems to me very much the sort of mythologizing wonderfully achieved in Canada in the work of writers of the 50's like Ann Wilkinson, Wilfred Watson, James Reaney—and, I would add, especially Irving Layton—those who took the traditional and rooted stories of western mythology and gave them a habitation and a name in those barren places of our imagination—Western Ontario, Winnipeg, Edmonton, Toronto and Downsview. A superb example is Layton's reworking of Greek myth and Nietzschian cultural criticism in "The Birth of Tragedy", a poem that provides a key to much of Layton's work. But that domestication of myth, if it *is* more than a technical tour de force, provides little more than an accommodation of contemporary experience to a long tradition of thought and feeling. I say "little more," which perhaps betrays a bias. What remains a mystery, I believe, is the point at which a literary mythology no longer serves its social functions. Too many others have written off cultures and announced the death of gods for anyone today to assume a prophetic mantle easily, and the kinds of social questions raised about technology and art seem to me far too complex for any kind of answer within the terms of this discussion. But the facts are observable and they extend at least to Kroetsch's version that "post-modern" means erasure, unwriting, the inversion of high and low culture. What we are to make of that is I think the major question Cohen's work raises. Another way to put this is to return to a concern I pointed to earlier in his work, one that becomes acute as he turns from high to low culture in response to the demands of audience: what connections could there possibly be between the dream of art and the reality of history?

Empson somewhere talks of Swift's discovery that everything high has a gross and low parody of it, the discovery that Norman O. Brown describes in his article "The Excremental Vision" in *Life Against Death*.[9] Cohen's identification of his sources and audience and his exploration of their meaning is of the same order: a Keatsian ode can be displaced into the diction, imagery, and rhythms of contemporary mass culture. The point of connection between art and history is fantasy. The demands of art and audience can be reconciled when nightmare becomes popular song, high becomes low, low high. A brilliant foreshadowing of what such inversions mean is Cohen's identification of artist and junkie, "Alexander Trocchi, Public Junkie, Priez Pour Nous." It begins, as you know:

> Who is purer
>   more simple than you?
> Priests play poker with the burghers
> police in underwear
>   leave Crime at the office,
> Our poets work bankers' hours
> retire to wives and fame reports.

The spike flashes in your blood
permanent as a silver lighthouse.
                    (*SP*, 108)

and continues with a contrast between Trocchi and the poet himself:

I'm apt to loaf
    in a coma of newspapers,
avoid the second-hand bodies
which cry to be catalogued.
I dream I'm
    a divine right Prime Minister,
I abandon plans for bloodshed in Canada.
I accept an O.B.E.

Under hard lights
with doctors' instruments
    you are at work
in the bathrooms of the city,
changing The Law.

I tend to get distracted
    by hydrogen bombs,
by Uncle's disapproval
    of my treachery
to the men's clothing industry.

I find myself
    believing public clocks,
taking advice
from the Dachau generation

The spike hunts
constant as a compass.
    You smile like a Navajo
discovering American oil
on his official slum wilderness,
a surprise every half hour.
                    (*SP*, 108-9)

The conclusion becomes obvious and paradoxical:

Your purity drives me to work.
I must get back to lust and microscopes,
experiments in embalming,
resume the census of my address book.

You leave behind you a fanatic
to answer RCMP questions.
                    (*SP*, 110)

The true artist—and saint—is the junkie: pure, focused, concentrated,
craftsman of need.

    The Trocchi poem prefigures *The Energy of Slaves* in theme and image but
not in tone or method, and from that point of view it is not fully realized,

a sensation rather than a real scandal. Between it and the genuine failure, something else had to intervene and that, of course, is *Beautiful Losers*. The point of this poetic novel is an ironic version of transformation: the ironic defense of the position of pop-hero, mass cult figure, is that he doesn't really exist; he has become an image, he has turned himself finally and formally into his art, he is a voice, a book, a radio, a vehicle spoken through rather than speaking. A neat trick, but unfortunately it didn't work. For whatever reason, *Beautiful Losers* seemed to both audience and critic confirmation of Cohen's mastery. Con-man, magician, scandal-monger, elusive charmer, he became more, not less evident, and all the flim-flummery of the book fooled no one. He had become that worst of all things, an artist. It is this double dialect then, "poems that drove me into poetry" and "women who keep driving me back into it,"[10] that remains unresolved and that occupies Cohen once more in *The Energy of Slaves*, a book about poetry, about enslavement, about politics.

Embarrassingly, the book raises a whole series of critical questions, many deliberately invited by Cohen himself, all of the most elementary kind, the sort usually handled with smug assurance by teachers of freshmen, the *Philistine* questions. Has he lost his talent? Or in a more vulgar form: is this poetry at all? Is this, as Cohen keeps insisting, the last feeble glimmering of a dying talent? "I'm no longer at my best practising/ the craft of verse"; he writes—or "Poetry begun in this mood rarely succeeds"; "Do you like this song?/I wrote it in a mood/that I would never/be seen dead in"; "Perhaps it is because my music/does not sing for me"; "That's why I can't write it anymore/I couldn't take the company";[11] and of course the lines most often quoted:

> I have no talent left
> I can't write a poem anymore
> You can call me Len or Lennie now
> like you always wanted
> (*ES*, 112)

Is poetry itself now impossible? Or in another series: are there some feelings that are simply anti-poetic or non-poetic? Self-pity? Hatred? Loathing? Disgust? Is there an authentic poetic language? Is it possible to write poetry about the impossibility of writing poetry? Is the dramatization of inauthenticity authentic? Is a genuinely inauthentic poem an authentic poem? And add to these: flat uninteresting structures, limp lines, flaccid diction, with just enough of a hint of the old lyric flair to reinforce the challenge to one's taste in such matters. The great classical structures of critical argument bear no relationship to this collapsed lyricism parading its limpness.

Two matters remain and bring this discussion to a close: one, the motif of slavery; the other, the assault on the audience or reader or "you" spoken to in the book. Both proceed, I believe, from the assumption of a betrayal common to both reader and poet. The first need not occupy us at length since it is the elaboration of the Trocchi point: slavery is defined simply as art and addiction. Art is opposed to work; it is habit, need, no longer the romanticized purity, focus, and concentration of the Trocchi poem, but the routine dreariness of meaningless necessary repetition. At the same time, the assault on the reader involves not only the poet's denial of talent but the reader's implication in the writer's own junky world. They stand in the relation of supplier to addict, feeding on each other's morbid necessities:

> Before you accuse me of boring you
> (your ultimate triumph and relief)
> remember neither you or me
> is fucking right now
> and once again you have enjoyed
> the company of my soul
> (*ES*, 112)

Another version of the dialectic appears: poet and audience, once in opposition to each other as art and history, now are coupled in opposition to life itself. This faked-up, hokey, tic-tackery of poems and songs, presenting itself as the imaginative revolution, calling on us to rouse up our faculties, now proves itself anything but the power of transformation. Its unity of being is seen finally as genitalia or mere mechanism of need, the unity of being hooked. The attack on culture implicit in the opposition between art and *real* wars, *real* love, *real* revolution is the more poignant in Cohen because he once believed in a perceptual revolution, because he once thought poetry was the front line, real politics. "This book," he once said of *Flowers for Hitler*, "moves me from this world of golden boy poet to the dung pile of the front-line writer."[12] Now, his mastery consists in taking the machine apart, bolt by bolt, to reveal it never worked anyhow.

Perhaps Cohen's argument simply provides fuel for those who would burn the poet anyway: it turns out, after all, that he deals in commonplaces, cliche's of contemporary thought, the detritus of cultural criticism, his language uninspired at that. But to say this is to spring the trap about which Cohen has been warning all along, even in his style. A double bind exists: condemn him and you are on the side of a now impossible refinement; join with him and you admit your complicity. The context of *The Energy of Slaves* is audience and politics; the persona, slave; the object now appears, paradoxically, as mastery or freedom. To be poet-master without being a poet-master.

The point is worth some elaboration, since it marks out the characteristic role assumed by the contemporary writer, "For God's sake, don't call it art." One means to achieve this ironic position, I've suggested, is disorganization; another, shifting of the field of reference from high to low, from elitist to popular forms; a third, perhaps the most subtle, consists of taking on any one of a variety of contemporary roles from junkie to madwoman to outlaw/forger or confidence man. Duplicity is far more characteristic of contemporary writing than either writer or reader seems willing to admit. Atwood's "This is a Photograph of Me," for example, opens out to possibilities that remain extraordinarily disturbing, especially since as the first poem in her first book it announces an obsessive concern. The photograph, we are told by the narrator in the same tone used to describe apparently objective features, "was taken/the day after I drowned/I am in the lake, in the centre/of the picture, just under the surface."[13] What are we to make of this? That a drowned woman is speaking to us? That the camera has subsumed her soul, drowned her? That the narrator, whose tone is so at odds with the situation, is insane? Or that the poem itself is a massive deception built on ambiguities inherent in structure, exploitable in diction? Or to take one other brief example, Ondaatje's *Billy the Kid*, warns of duplicity in "photographs," exploits forgeries, anachronism, and deception; and his passionate, loving, and controlled meditation on a photograph of his adolescence, "Burning Hills," ends with the astonishing lines that offer, if not an explanation, at least the questions to be asked:

When he finishes he will go back
hunting for the lies that are obvious.[14]

What lies? *Only* the obvious ones? Are there others? Will any be changed or only discovered by the poet, left there for our own bemusement?

In *The Modern Century,* Northrop Frye links the criminal-saint and outlaw figure with a tradition in American pastoral, on the one hand, of the artist as hobo and bum, and in European romanticism, on the other, of artist as bohemian and confidence man, and I suppose, as Frye notes, Cohen's work belongs there, as does Atwood's or Ondaatje's. But to notice the traditional features of the role does not, I think, answer to its contemporary implications. Cervantes wrote in the 16th century at the very moment when, as Leo Spitzer observes, the power of literacy manifested itself in the new humanism.[15] One possible reading of the *Don Quixote* is as an ironic attack on the dissolution of reality in the medium of print. That Cervantes' attack on books is itself in a book is surely additional and intended irony. That the meaning of imagination has been a perennial problem for *writers* in no way lessens the significance of a contemporary critique of high culture. Given a particular technology, the ghost of Cervantes may have more, not less, reason for living today than at any time since he first wrote.

My point has been mainly to explicate, to put Cohen's book in the context of a culture which in part he helped to create. But I would go further: *The Energy of Slaves* remains valuable because it elucidates with the precision we used to call poetry the failure of contemporary poetry. Far more uncompromising than Lee or Atwood or Bowering or Ondaatje, and more scrupulous, Cohen is equally more compromised than all of them because closer to each of us, that is, to the duplicity of consciousness and history. His development as a writer illustrates, as it creates, one of the main lines of development in Canadian writing, the gradual realization that art has the capacity to contain its own contradiction. *The Energy of Slaves* has the inevitability of fated writing; it was inherent in Cohen's understanding of contemporary imagination (i.e. his audience) and his awareness of the infinite regressiveness of personality, "all this endless reconsidering,"[16] as Philip Roth says about novelists; it was inherent too, we can now understand, in the first words a young poet wrote about a drowned god or in the lyric lines about a clever corpse in a love-soaked bed or in the urging of an imaginative revolutionary like a manic P.M. in Cuba to his brothers to join him governing this country. That poem is called "The Only Tourist in Havana Turns His Thoughts Homeward" and I conclude with its splendid and lunatic anarchy:

> Come, my brothers,
> let us govern Canada,
> let us find our serious heads,
> let us dump asbestos on the White House,
> let us make the French talk English,
>   not only here but everywhere,
> let us torture the Senate individually
>   until they confess,
> let us purge the New Party,
> let us encourage the dark races
>   so they'll be lenient
>   when they take over,
> let us make the CBC talk English. . . .
> let us have another official language,
> let us determine what it will be,
> let us give a Canada Council Fellowship
>   to the most original suggestion,
> let us teach sex in the home
>   to parents,
> let us threaten to join the U.S.A.
>   and pull out at the last moment,
> my brothers, come,
> our serious heads are waiting for us somewhere
>   like Gladstone bags abandoned
>   after a *coup d'etat*,
> let us put them on very quickly,
> let us maintain a stony silence
>   on the St. Lawrence Seaway.
>   Havana, April 1961 (*SP*, 104)

NOTES

1. George Steiner, *Language & Silence* (New York: Atheneum 1967), p. 10.

2. *Ibid.*, p. 10.

3. Northrop Frye, *The Modern Century* (Toronto: Oxford University Press, 1967), p. 85.

4. *Ibid.*, p. 104.

5. W.A. Johnsen, "Toward a Redefinition of Modernism", *Boundary/2*, Vol. II, No. 3, Spring 1974, p. 543.

6. Robert Kroetsch, "Preface To Canadian Edition", *Boundary/2*, Vol. III, No. 1, Fall 1974, p. 1.

7. Leonard Cohen, *Selected Poems* (Toronto: McClelland & Stewart, 1968), p. 57.

8. A.M. Klein, "Portrait of the Poet as Landscape", *Collected Poems* (Toronto: McGraw Hill, 1974), pp. 334-335.

9. N.O. Brown, "The Excremental Vision", *Life Against Death* (Wesleyan University Press, 1963), pp. 179-201.

10. Leonard Cohen, *The Energy of Slaves* (Toronto: McClelland and Stewart, 1972), pp. 14, 112.

11. *Ibid.*, pp. 24, 18, 56, 74, 107.

12. Leonard Cohen, *Flowers for Hitler* (Toronto: McClelland and Stewart, 1964), blurb on back cover.

13. Margaret Atwood, "This is a Photograph of Me", *The Circle Game* (Toronto: Contact Press, 1966), p. 11.

14. Michael Ondaatje, *Rat Jelly* (Toronto: Coach House Press, 1973), p. 58.

15. Leo Spitzer, "On the Significance of Don Quijote", ed. Lowry Nelson Jr., *Cervantes* (New Jersey: Prentice Hall, 1969), pp. 85-86.

16. Ann Mandel, "Useful Fictions: Legends of the Self in Roth, Blaise, Kroetsch, and Nowlan", *The Ontario Review*, No. 3, Fall-Winter 1975-1976, p. 32.

Atwood
Gothic

Margaret Atwood's *You Are Happy* offers not only her usual poetic transformations, identifications, witch-woman figures, animal-men, and pho-
tograph-poems but also an intriguing set of "Tricks with Mirrors." It is
the mirror poems that suggest, more pointedly than usual in her work,
questions about duplicity and reflexiveness—concerns quite different
from apparently clear and accessible social comment. She writes:

> Don't assume it is passive
> or easy, this clarity
>
> with which I give you yourself,
> Consider what restraint it
>
> takes. . . .
>
> It is not a trick either,
>
> It is a craft:
> mirrors are crafty.
>
> . . . .
>
> You don't like these metaphors
> All right:
>
> Perhaps I am not a mirror.
> Perhaps I am a pool.
>
> Think about pools. (pp. 26-27)

Quite likely the speaker of the poem is meant to be taken as a lover;
certainly she speaks to a Narcissus gazing at her as if she were a mirror;
and to hear in the voice the artist's warning about craftiness may seem
perverse, though the suggestion of allegory is so tempting in Atwood's
works it is difficult to resist. In any event, the mirror voice does present

ambiguous possibilities that call to mind apparently contradictory qualities in Atwood's writing: clarity and accessibility, certainly, combined
with extraordinary deftness in manipulating contemporary modes of
speech and image, and a compelling toughmindedness, a ruthless unsen-
timentality, which is somehow liberating rather than cynically enclosing.
These modes and attitudes point to social concerns, but one senses that
as surface qualities these may be concealing quite different interests. It is
not my intention to deny the obvious, that she does handle with force
and insight important contemporary social metaphors: the politics of
love and self, the mystification of experience, woman as prisoner of the
mind police, social institutions as models of the police state, the schizophrenic journey toward health, and so on. But the oracular qualities of
her work, no doubt as attractive as social commentary to her readers,
deserve more extended commentary than they have received. I am
thinking of the gothic elements of her novels, her consistent and obsessive use of reduplicating images, and her totemic animal imagery.

Margaret Atwood's comment, in a conversation with Graeme Gibson,
that *Surfacing* "is a ghost story" provides the point of departure for more
than one commentary on her work. Less often noticed is the special form
of ghost story Atwood employs, the story in *Journals of Susanna Moodie*, for
example. Mrs. Moodie appears to Atwood, we are told, in a dream, later
manifesting herself to the poet "as a mad-looking and very elderly lady";
the poems take her "through an estranged old age, into death and
beyond." (p. 63) That makes her a ghost in the last poem, "A Bus Along
St. Clair: December," where she tells us:

> I am the old woman
> sitting across from you on the bus,
> her shoulders drawn up like a shawl;
> out of her eyes come secret
> hatpins, destroying
> the walls, the ceiling.
> (p. 61)

Her earthly life, portrayed in the earlier poems, involves a pattern not
unlike the heroine's journey into the backwoods in *Surfacing*: a landing on
a seashore apparently occupied by dancing sandflies, a pathway into a
forest, confrontation with a wolfman and other animals, men in masks,
deaths of children, including a drowning, sinister plants. Gothic tale is a
better name than ghost story for this form, in which the chief element is
the threat to a maiden, a young girl, a woman. In a well-known passage,
Leslie Fiedler, (allegorizing like mad, incidentally), comments on the
chief features of the form, its motifs:

> Chief of the gothic symbols is, of course, the Maiden in flight. . . . Not
> the violation or death which sets such a flight in motion, but the flight
> itself figures forth the essential meaning of the anti-bourgeois gothic,
> for which the girl on the run and her pursuer become only alternate

versions of the same plight. Neither can come to rest before the other—for each is the projection of his opposite . . . actors in a drama which depends on both for its significance. Reinforcing the meaning . . . is the haunted countryside, and especially the haunted castle or abbey which rises in its midst, and in whose dark passages and cavernous apartments the chase reaches its climax.[1]

Substitute forest for haunted castle, and think of the ghosts of Mrs. Radcliffe's *The Italian,* and the ghost story or gothic form of an Atwood poem or novel begins to take shape. Obviously, it is richly suggestive of a variety of dark threats, either psychological or hidden in the social structure. Atwood's own political and social commentary on Canadian imagination employs, with superb wit and skill, a victor/victim pattern (the haunted victim, the haunted persecutor, perhaps?) to outline not only an endlessly repeated pattern, but a theory of colonialism, that is, victimization. We see the possibilities: if *Surfacing* presents itself as political and social criticism disguised as ghost story, could it be that *Survival* takes its unusual power precisely from the fact that it is a ghost story disguised as politics and criticism?

A further elaboration is suggested by Ellen Moers' comments in the chapter of *Literary Women* called "The Female Gothic": Gothic, says Moers, is writing that "has to do with fear," writing in which "fantasy predominates over reality, the strange over the commonplace, and the supernatural over the natural, with one definite auctorial intent: to scare. Not, that is, to reach down into the depths of the soul and purge it with pity and terror (as we say tragedy does), but to get to the body itself, its glands, muscles, epidermis, and circulatory system, quickly arousing and quickly allaying the physiological reactions to fear."[2] Moers' emphasis on physiological effect seems appropriate. It points to the kind of imagination found, say, in Michael Ondaatje's work as well as in Atwood's that might appropriately be called a physiological imagination, whose purpose is evident.[3]

Fear. But fear of what? Some say sexuality, especially taboo aspects of sexuality, incest for example: the gothic threat to a young woman carries implications of sado-masochistic fantasy, the victim/victor pattern of *Survival.* Ellen Moers suggests that in Mary Shelley's *Frankenstein,* the real taboo is birth itself: death and birth are hideously mixed in the creation of a monster out of pieces of the human body. (The image involves, as well, the hideousness of duplication and reduplication.) In Atwood's "Speeches for Dr. Frankenstein," her Dr. Frankenstein addresses his creation in unmistakable language about a botched creation, a birth/death confusion:

I was insane with skill:
I made you perfect.

I should have chosen instead
to curl you small as a seed,

trusted beginnings. Now I wince
before this plateful of results:

core and rind, the flesh between
already turning rotten.

I stand in the presence
of the destroyed god:

A rubble of tendons,
knuckles and raw sinews.

Knowing that the work is mine
How can I love you?
(*The Animals in That Country*, p. 44)

If, as he says to his monster, Dr. Frankenstein might have trusted in beginnings, in seed, the narrator of *Surfacing*, it seems, distrusts virtually all births. How much of the haunting proceeds from an abortion? We discern a pattern of mixed birth/death in the book: the baby not born, the baby aborted, the baby about to be born as a furred monster, the drowned brother who didn't drown, the baby peering out of the mother's stomach, the embryo-like frogs, the frog-like embryo, the man-frog father in the waters, hanging from the camera with which he might have photographed the gods.

Who are the ghosts of *Surfacing* then? In *Survival*, which reads like a gloss on *Surfacing*, Atwood tells us that the ghost or death goddess of *The Double Hook* represents fear, but not fear of death, fear of life. And babies? Following a rather horrendous list of miscarriages, cancers, tumours, stillbirths and worse, which she finds in Canadian novels, Atwood remarks laconically, "The Great Canadian Baby is sometimes alarmingly close to the Great Canadian Coffin." (p. 208) Who are the ghosts of *Surfacing*? A mother, a father, a lost child, Indians, the animals: all symbols of vitality, life, our real humanity, that has disappeared and must be brought back. "It does not approve of me or disapprove of me," the narrator says of the creature who is elemental, as she thinks her father has become: "it tells me it has nothing to tell me, only the fact of itself." (p. 187) And she says of her parents after her paroxysm in the woods: "they dwindle, grow, become what they were, human. Something I never gave them credit for." (p. 189) Ghosts: only the human body, repressed, denied; only life denied. All proceeds from the ghosts: a de-realized world: victimization, sexism, deformed sexuality, sado-masochism, tearing away at nature's body, at our own bodies.

But to say this is to accept the *allegory* of gothic that Atwood allows her narrator to spell out for us (it is worth noting that in the best gothic fashion, the daylight world after the horrors of the long night reveals that the ghosts are mechanical or waxwork figures). To say this is also to explain away not only the ghosts but one of the most disturbing and most characteristic of Atwood's qualities, her sense of doubleness, of reduplication, in word and image. Even the victor/victim pattern recurs and the tale told once in *Surfacing* will be told again. At the end, nothing is resolved.

The ghosts are sexual fears, repressed contents of the imagination, social rigidity. They are also literary images, book reflections, patterns from all those readings in gothic romance, perhaps even the unwritten thesis Atwood proposed for her Ph.D., on gothic romance. Reduplication. Margaret Atwood's first book of poetry bears the title *Double Persephone*. The first poem of *The Circle Game* is called "This is a photograph of Me," and the speaker tells us that if you look closely at the lake, you will discern her image; in parenthesis we are told:

(The photograph was taken
the day after I drowned.

I am in the lake, in the centre
of the picture, just under the surface.

It is difficult to say where
precisely, or to say
how large or small I am:
the effect of water
on light is a distortion

but if you look long enough,
eventually
you will be able to see me.)
(p. 11)

End of brackets. A kind of insane phenomenology takes over that precise meticulous speech; we enter a world of reflections within reflections, totemic duplication (consider the possibilities in the simple four-part structure: man masked; man unmasked; animal masked; animal unmasked) and de-realized experience. Mirror, water and reflection, games like cards and chess, maps or models, eyes and cameras make up the major duplications, though there are more subtle ones in births and ghosts, in movies, photographs, drownings, archeology, astral travel, revenants, echoes, icons, comic books and gardens. The list, I think, could be extended—or duplicated—but its obsessive nature should be clear. It should also be clear that the list points up the literary nature of Atwood's concerns, otherwise fairly successfully disguised by her field of reference, popular and contemporary imagery. In *You Are Happy*, a poem called "Gothic Letter on a Hot Night" gives, in a typically wry and throw-away manner, the reflexive pattern of story within story. Presumably this speaker faces a blank page and longs for stories again, but it is not clear whether that is bad (she ought not to live her life in stories) or good (she cannot write and therefore all the bad things the stories could do will remain undone). Either way, there is a sinister suggestion that the stories (like the poem one writes to drown one's sister, or the things that go on just outside the frame of the picture, the part you cannot see) will in fact, or could in fact, write the lives of the story-teller:

> It was the addiction
> to stories, every
> story about herself or anyone
> led to the sabotage of each address
> and all those kidnappings
>
> Stories that could be told
> on nights like these to account for the losses
> litanies of escapes, bad novels, thrillers
> deficient in villains;
> now there is nothing to write
> She would have given almost anything
> to have them back,
> those destroyed houses, smashed plates, calendars.
>
> (p. 15)

An ambiguity, unresolved, is that the poem begins in first person but in the second stanza shifts to third person narrative. The three—the "I" speaking, the "you" addressed, and the "she" who tells stories—remain unidentified. Duplicity, in part, consists in trying to have it both ways. No doubt, Atwood would recoil from my reading backwards to the material from which she begins, and which often seems to form the object of her irony: don't live in stories, you are not literature, if you think you would like it when the gods do reveal themselves try it sometime. So *Surfacing* moves from the world of ghosts back to the place where the narrator can be seen for what she is, a poor naked shivering wretch, scarcely human. But the ambiguity is in the power of the material. *You Are Happy* ends with what looks like a dismissal of "the gods and their static demands," but leaves open the question—again—whether you can only do this if you have been there, have known them. Even in parody and irony (let alone social comments on literary forms) the problem, the puzzle about reduplication remains.

A similar question arises with Robertson Davies' *World of Wonders*; that is, should we read it psychologically, in Jungian terms, as Davies intends, or theatrically, as a series of beautifully structured and terribly inflated poses, or magically, as not only the charlatan's illusions but the magician's powers. This question is somewhere in the background of Michael Ondaatje's *The Collected Works of Billy the Kid* (all the deceit, the obvious lies, as Ondaatje says of another poem) and in Kroetsch's insistent attempt to uninvent the world he wants so desperately to be at home in. Perhaps the disclaimers are essential to the magic of repetition, a kind of Borgesian pretence that the story or poem is really an essay, or that the essay is a story. The problem is, whatever philosophic dilemmas duplication raises about time and cause, psychologically and poetically it seems far more sinister than the writer wishes to admit. Either a fraud or a magician, the crude choice would seem to be. To which we answer (and this involves the reduplication) neither: this is only a story about both.

Psychologically, as Borges points out in *Labyrinths,* the story of a world created by a written version of another world of endless reduplication, of halls of mirrors, is a horror. "Mirrors have something monstrous about them . . . because they increase the number of men."[4] In folklore, the doppleganger motif, in which one meets oneself coming back as one goes forward, signifies either death or the onset of prophetic power. In Jung's commentary on the *I Ching,* synchronicity substitutes chance for cause, a randomness that plays havoc with notions of identity and opens the possibility of occult possession. The vegetable version of this pattern, in its benign form, is sacramental, and in its malign or demonic form, cannibalistic. Atwood's ironic awareness of such patterns pervades her humanized gardens and provides a structural principle for her novel, *The Edible Woman.* But whatever the psychological significance, the literary seems more difficult for her; for in literary terms, as Borges argues, the device of reduplication calls attention to the poem and hence to the fictional nature of the poem's reality. It de-realizes experience:

Why does it disturb us that the map be included in the map and the thousand and one nights in the book of the *Thousand and One Nights?* Why does it disturb us that Don Quixote be a reader of the *Quixote* and Hamlet a spectator of *Hamlet?* . . . The inversions suggest that if the characters of a fictional work can be readers and spectators, we, its readers or spectators, can be fictitious. In 1833, Carlyle observed that the history of the universe is an infinite sacred book that all men write and read and try to understand, and in which they are also written.[5]

Borges remarks that tales of fantasy are not haphazard combinations: "They have a meaning, they make us feel that we are living in a strange world."[6] Focusing on the obvious, the map of Canada in a tourist agency, viewed by a window lady who sees her own reflection containing the mapped country, Atwood gives us a country stranger than we knew:

look, here, Saskatchewan
is a flat lake, some convenient rocks
where two children pose with a father
and the mother is cooking something
in immaculate slacks by a smokeless fire,
her teeth white as detergent.

Whose dream is this, I would like to know:

  . . .   .

Unsuspecting
window lady, I ask you:

143

Do you see nothing
watching from under the water?

Was the sky ever that blue?

Who really lives there?
                    ("At the Tourist Centre in Boston")

Borges' temptation is solipsism (think of your life as a dream). But
Atwood's poem characteristically questions the dream. No matter that
this is the American dream of Canada, "A manufactured hallucination";
the Unsuspecting Reflection, water and sky in her own head, doesn't
surface, lives with her unanswered questions.

It would be possible, I suppose, to read Atwood's career as a search for
techniques to answer those questions honestly, resolve the reflecting/
reflector dilemma by demystifying experience. Certainly by the time of
Power Politics she attained an impressive command of deflating ironies; a
poem like "They Eat Out" sets up opposing stereotypes of magical
thinking in an atmosphere of fried rice and pop culture:

I raise the magic fork
over the plate of beef fried rice

and plunge it into your heart.
There is a faint pop, a sizzle

and through your own split head
you rise up glowing;

the ceiling opens
a voice sings Love is a Many

Splendoured Thing
you hang suspended above the city

in blue tights and red cape,
your eyes flashing in unison.

. . .   .

As for me, I continue eating;
I liked you better the way you were
but you were always ambitious.

But writing has its own power, its metaphors, like mirrors in the language. No one knows what word the heroine of *Surfacing* will speak first.
It is possible that she will say nothing. Silence can be the strategy of those
who have endured. But if there is any sense to my argument that
Atwood's obsessive concern with mirror and reflection is an attempt to
resolve an impossible dilemma about writing and experience, or about
fiction and wisdom; and at the same time, a sort of playing about with the

fires of magical possession, then I would guess that tormented girl would turn towards us and say:

> You don't like these metaphors
> All right
> Think about pools.

NOTES

1. Leslie Fiedler, *Love and Death in The American Novel* (New York: Meridian Books, 1962), pp. 111-112.

2. Ellen Moers, *Literary Women* (New York: Doubleday and Company, 1976), p. 90.

3. Like Atwood, Ondaatje, especially in *The Collected Works of Billy the Kid,* and Robert Kroetsch in *The Studhorse Man* and *Badlands,* tend to bring together images of sexuality, dismemberment, and poetics, poetic and sexual obsessions leading to anatomies.

4. Jorge Luis Borges, "Tlon, Uqbar, Orbes Tertius", *Labyrinths* (New York: New Directions, 1962), p. 3.

5. Jorge Luis Borges, "Partial Magic in the Quixote", *Labyrinths,* p. 196.

6. Jorge Luis Borges, "Tales of the Fantastic", *Prism International,* Vol. 8, No. 1, (Summer, 1968), p. 15.

Criticism
as
Ghost Story

"First draw four leaves. They should vary in length. A fifth leaf crosses them. In this there is grace and beauty. . . . Ink tones should be varied. Old and young leaves should mingle. Petals should be light, stamens and calyx dark. The hand should move like lightning; it should never be slow or hesitant."[1] These are words translated from *The Mustard Seed Garden Manual of Painting*, "a Chinese standard textbook on painting from the seventeenth century,"[2] and as W.H. Gombrich tells us in his study of the psychology of pictorial representation, *Art and Illusion*, not only do they constitute rules summarized in traditional four word phrases which the disciple memorized by chanting but

> There is nothing in Western art which compares with this conception
> of painting; indeed, the language in which we discuss pictures differs
> so radically from the critical terminology of the Far East that all
> attempts to translate from one into the other are frustrated by this
> basic difference of categories.[3]

Just so. But *The Mustard Seed Garden Manual of Painting*—or rather, its inaccessibility—presents, as the schematized flower does, the very problem in criticism to which this paper is directed. We seem to have no difficulty in discerning as a vocabulary of pictorial art geometrical forms within or informing paintings, and if we are among those fascinated by alphabets of the imagination, we might even follow Gombrich so far as to agree that lifelikeness or representation constitutes little more than, in his words, "dreams for those who are awake."[4] But with the languages of poetry and fiction, and particularly with the language of criticism, it is otherwise, or so we want to say, or even more precisely, so at least most Canadian critics of Canadian writers would want to say.

By now it should be perfectly obvious that this is not intended to be even the sketchiest summary of the kinds and varieties of Canadian criticism. For those who seek that there are available useful accounts, Clara Thomas's *Seeing Niagara and After*, for example, or Miriam Waddington's survey of recent criticism in the *Supplement* to the *Oxford Companion to Canadian History and Literature*. Nor will the question of a national criticism or of nationalism itself occupy me, though it is a question intensely debated at the moment in Canada. It is rather at the present moment than the beginning of Canadian literary criticism that I want this discussion to start, and that point, for a variety of fascinating and puzzling reasons is Margaret Atwood's *Survival: a Thematic Guide to Canadian Literature*.

It is not likely that there will be any serious disagreement with Professor Waddington's view that Canadian literary criticism has concerned itself largely with interpretations of the shaping forces of geography, biculturalism, and colonialism in Canadian life and writing. But whatever varying degrees of emphasis may have been put upon the question of primary imaginative focus, the social context almost invariably dissolves into the geographical, that in its own turn becoming the core of a mythic, rather than empirical or historical, response. To the extent that Atwood's *Survival* presents another version of the myth of the land in Canadian writing, it presents us with nothing surprising or new, and at a glance one could only account for its phenomenal presence and import in political terms: its radical and aggressive nationalism appealing to a shared national mood. But this, it seems to me, is a trivial way of putting a rather more serious question: in what sense could a thematic or mythic version of a national literature be taken as serious social comment? *Survival* brings into question the meaning and nature of all earlier attempts at a sociology of literature in Canadian writing, precisely because its social and historical awareness appear as frail, to use Professor Waddington's words, "as the metaphysical structure [it employs] to deal with the vast array of historical and empirical facts that must be dealt with in any consideration of the present situation in Canadian literature."[5]

To put the point rather more sharply than I would ordinarily want to: Atwood's *Survival* stands at one end of a developing line of thematic and cultural criticism in Canada and in direct opposition to the kinds of literary sociology implied in the work of critics like George Woodcock, A.J.M. Smith, Desmond Pacey, or Ronald Sutherland. It is a classic mistake, of course, to regard Northrop Frye as the sole defining force in the creation of a kind of Canadian cultural Freudianism. Powerful and influential though his essays may have been, they must be put alongside the equally important socio-cultural analyses by Marshall McLuhan, James Reaney, Milton Wilson, Warren Tallman, D.G. Jones, and Irving Layton. The list is not random. Like the names in the dedication to *Survival*, it suggests that a peculiarly literary version of Canadian personality has been developing for some time in critical and theoretical discussions of Canadian writing. Its relationship to our history may be judged by comparing the equally mythic accounts of personality and society which can be discerned in the work of historians like W.L. Morton,

Donald Creighton, and William Kilbourn. My own favourite example has long been that splendid passage in which W.L. Morton presents as historical reality a version of Canadian life that would have delighted Leo Marx for its extraordinarily precise correspondence to his own sense of pastoral:

> this alternate penetration of the wilderness and return of civilization is the basic element of Canadian character whether French or English, the violence necessary to contend with the wilderness, the restraint necessary to preserve civilization from the wilderness violence, and the puritanism which is the offspring of the wedding of violence to restraint. Even in an industrial and urban society the old rhythm continues, for the typical Canadian holiday is a wilderness holiday, whether among the lakes of the Sheild or the peaks of the Rockies.[6]

From Creighton to Kilbourn and beyond, our historians have been writing Canadian history as novel, and for this reason it seemed to me essential to represent them in *Contexts of Canadian Criticism*. Their sense of history as the art of narration, to use Creighton's phrase, far exceeds our critics' sense that, as Oscar Wilde would have it, the critic is artist, a teller of tales.

If such remarks were indeed scandalous, one could only reflect sadly on the peculiarities of Canadian writers. It is true, no doubt, that far deeper wounds than told in any fictions have been incurred in Canadian life, but what remains to be told, and I put this as a painful question, is whether the sociology of either critics or historians in this country has been or indeed could be adequate to those wounds, that suffering. How presumptuous, after all, our efforts turn out to be. Atwood's *Survival* spreading out before us image upon image of broken bodies, we are told, is just a story, the victor/victim pattern an imposed structure. This is not literary criticism, so one of the complaints runs, because it is too much like a novel: "It has many of the features of a novel. . . . Poems and novels have their own logic, different from that found in critical discourse. . . . Since it is never possible to argue with images, and since *Survival* consists almost entirely of metaphors and images, all critical discussions of the problems it considers is ruled out."[7]

But this is the crux: are there indeed those levels of discourse that separate novelist and critic, and to whom then does the authority, especially with respect to those extraordinarily imposing facts of social and historical life, attach? Could it be that *Survival* takes its unusual power precisely from the fact that it is criticism as novel, as ghost story disguised as politics and criticism? With all those Canadian corpses around in our poems and novels, what Boston strangler has been let loose in Toronto or Regina? Who is that dark, fierce figure pursuing a maiden endlessly across the waste landscape? At the basis of the gothic tale is a sado-masochistic sexual fantasy, Atwood's name for which is the victor/victim pattern. If you want to politicize the tale, talk of American

imperialism and Canadian colonial victims, but if you want to understand its power as a focusing lens of Canadian social life, you must think
not of mythic magic but of the analytic or logical powers of myth.
Commenting on the cultural anthropology of Levi-Strauss, or indeed
analyzing the social structure of the Babar stories, Edmund Leach notes
two characteristic features of myth: redundancy and a markedly binary
aspect; that is, myths tell the same story over and over again, and always
a story involving a dualism resolved by a monstrous or holy third. In the
language of systems engineers, "a high level of redundancy makes it easy
to correct errors introduced by noise";[8] the relevance to Atwood's victor/
victim pattern should be immediately apparent as indeed its power as a
structural feature of Canadian life.

Atwood's *Survival* tells a ghost story and is superb criticism because it
seeks its sociology in language and not in history or society. Whatever its
flaws of wit and irony and even superciliousness, it relentlessly main-
tains its hold of our being in the syntax of our lives. I have not, I trust,
chosen the phrase idly. As opposed to notions of environment, of biculturalism, geography, imperial power, I place a question of syntax. It
would be ludicrous, I suppose, to argue this distinction in places of
political power, but its meaning for those places ought by now to be clear
enough. If we need to be reminded, there is one critic who has consistently addressed himself to the subtle and disturbing questions of the
real links between language, culture, and power. It is George Steiner
whose essays *In Blue Beard's Castle* trace out once again the consequences
of what he calls elsewhere "the retreat from the word":[9]

> We empty of their humanity those to whom we deny speech. We make
> them naked and absurd. There is a terrible, literal image in 'stone
> deafness', in the opaque babble and speechlessness of the 'stoned'.
> Break off speech to others and the Medusa turns inward. . . . Deliber-
> ate violence is being done to those primary ties of identity and social
> cohesion produced by a common language.[10]

It is profoundly within what Steiner calls "the sinews of Western speech"[11]
that we find "the forces and valuations prevailing in the body politic,"[12]
the identity of the social and linguistic orders, the texture and felt depth
of language as the very fabric of society itself.

To deny the primacy of language in literacy, in a literate, a word
culture, denies that culture itself, but this is a simplistic formulation,
because the nature of the denial needs to be told. Most sociological
criticism seeks to formulate the linguistic, the language problem simply
as a problem of elegant reference. That it might be our body, our
imagination, our culture, and hence our society, seems to have occurred
to few indeed.

The beginning of criticism, I begin by saying, might be *The Chinese
Mustard Seed Catalogue*. At the end, I can only point quickly to those who

might now be writing a Canadian version. W.H. New in his *Articulating West,* a title chosen with some care I think, distinguishes between those of our writers who sought to find a language appropriate to a landscape and those who are now, exploring, in his words "the landscape that is language itself, for the purpose of freeing the imagination from representational strictures and affirming the compatibility of spiritual (visionary) and political (empirical) goals."[13] That could be the programme for 'survival'. It is without question the concern of critics like Gloria Onley and Robert McDougall and poets like B.P. Nichol and Stephen McCaffrey. Writing in *Open Letter,* McCaffrey and Nichol turn their attention to problems of translation, a guise for writing about the relationship between letter and pictogram; that relationship, we are told, is geomantic, because of its similarity to the art of geomancy as practiced in ancient China and by the lost builders of Stonehenge. No doubt, it will seem to some incongruous to reach the end of a discussion of Canadian literary criticism with the notion that we ought to build Stonehenge in Ontario's green and pleasant land, but the exigencies of 'survival' are many and mysterious. And if nothing else, our youngest critics will at least remind us that we had best look once more at the words themselves that spell out desire, dream, our bodies' love for all the life of the world.

NOTES

1. E.H. Gombrich, *Art and Illusion* (London: Phaidon Press, 1972), p. 129.

2. *Ibid.,* p. 128.

3. *Ibid.,* p. 129.

4. *Ibid.,* p. 127.

5. Miriam Waddington, "Literary Studies in English", *Supplement to the Oxford Companion to Canadian History and Literature,* p. 206.

6. W.L. Morton, *The Canadian Identity* (Toronto: University of Toronto Press, 1972), p. 5.

7. Waddington, p. 206.

8. E. Leach, "Genesis as Myth", ed. V.W. Gras, *European Literary Theory and Practice* (New York: Dell Publishing, 1973), p. 318.

9. George Steiner, *Language and Silence* (New York: Atheneum, 1967), pp. 12-36.

10. George Steiner, *In Bluebeard's Castle* (New Haven: Yale University Press, 1971), p. 111.

11. *Ibid.,* p. 88.

12. *Ibid.*

13. W.H. New, *Articulating West* (Toronto: New Press, 1972), p. xxiv.

Banff:
The Magic Mountain

I THE PHENOMENOLOGY OF MOUNTAINS

And then he thinks he knows
The hills where his life rose
And the sea where it goes
                    Matthew Arnold

What makes the mountains high in the first place is not entirely understood

        A Guide to Geology for Visitors to Canada's National Parks

Mountain: a natural elevation of the earth's surface, rising notably
        above the surrounding level and attaining an altitude
        which, relative to adjacent elevations, is impressive
                                                    OED

        Scenery Is Everywhere Changing
                                A Guide to Geology

                a region remote from civilization
                                        OED

        That day, the last of my youth, on the last of our mountains
                                            Earle Birney

We sat there, on the wood deck overlooking the slope to the town and
across the river and the woods on the other side to the great ranges, and
talked and talked in the summer heat. Words. Birney's "David". *Rocky
Mountain Foot, Rivers among Rocks.* Is that the right title? Gustafson's book.
How many or how few books on mountains do you know? They were
still talking, on the deck. Shadows. Something about magicians in Lub-
lin.

151

Paranoia. The writer's illness. It's in the words. Because saying them turns you on, turns them on. All around me, writers, busily turning the world into words. Each day arriving at the writing programme seminar with pages and pages of "free fall," the confessional stain, the blurb, blur, burr, blear, rare:

surrounded by the mountains. You'd think by now I'd know their names, their directions, could give you the geology.

In Cuzco, at 11,500 feet, you move from the plane at the airport alongside your wife, daughters, as in a dream of slow motion, slight dizziness, tightness around the chest, the air washed bright, the sun bright but not at the level you expect and not as warm as it should be. Toward Juliaco, on the train, climbing. 13,500 feet: the Altiplano, climbing. Entry in Peruvian Journal:

August 20 at the National Museum I make these notes: Funerary Trusseau pertaining to same tomb. . . . Sumptuary Objects: shell necklaces (hualca). Metal Shawl Pins (tupus) teeth from wooden combs (nacchu) 14 carved shell fish with inset green stone eyes.

Inca Ceramics:

—Interstice (lageneria vulgaris) of the cucupitaceas family with metal incrustations on it representing birds and faces of felines—

Pictographic porcelain

clubs in the form of stars (champas)

an egg-shaped weapon made with spikes

Mummies at the National Museum: Cuzco

A female Inca Mummy for the most part covered in braided straw. Fingernails can be seen on both hands.

A male Inca Mummy in a perfect state of preservation with ears, eyes, and fingernails intact.

How to arrive at Banff: by plane from Edmonton to Calgary, bus to
Banff, taxi to school

by car from Wabamun to Jasper to Banff
(stops at Edson and Hinton) on the
Banff-Jasper Highway: stops at Athabaska falls,
at Sunwapta Falls, at Columbia Ice-fields,
to School

by plane from Vancouver to Saskatoon by bus
to Calgary (lunch at Tisdale Sask, of green
peas and breaded-veal-cutlet sandwich) at
Calgary taxi to Banff school arriving 3:00
am. total elapsed time: 15 hours.

thunderstorms on the prairies

by train from Toronto to Edmonton
by plane from Toronto to Edmonton

by plane from Toronto to Calgary
by plane from Edmonton to Calgary
by bus from Saskatoon to Calgary
bus
car
taxi

enter the mountains

The Banff Centre is situated about half way up Tunnel Mountain overlooking the town of Banff.[1] It consists of central hall and administration building with its theatre, reading rooms, offices, lobbies, dining halls, and partly circling it chalets, an art building, a theatre. It is the summer location of a school of fine arts, including teaching in music, dance, photography, painting, theatre, writing. It presents an annual festival of the arts, ballet, musical comedy, opera, musical concerts. On the lawn in front of the administration building, Donald Cameron Hall, hamburgers are served at noon, the mountains in the central foreground, the Bow River moving toward its falls below the Banff Springs Hotel. In a church basement in the town, a few people sitting on folding chairs will watch a reading of "The Jones Boy," the readers at a table on raised stage. The students of the writing class meet in the morning to hear readings from "free fall," unstructured impressions they have been putting down on pages as rapidly as possible the day before. There is some comment, laughter.

In the sun-room where a bar opens at four in the afternoon, over a growing and building sound volume the Olympics struggle to make themselves visible through the micro-wave barrier of the mountains, the television image twisting into triple and quadruple exposures and bands of green, blue, and violet to the accompanied mutter of commentary and aside, the star system momentarily focusing on something other than its own concerns of acting, writing, dancing, playing, singing, for there is no mistake here in the mountains about the nature of elevation: this is high, this is a high: a natural elevation of, rising notably above, attaining an altitude which . . . is: *impressive*.

> Summer surprised us, coming over the Starnbergersee
> With a shower of rain; we stopped in the colonnade,
> And went on in sunlight, into the Hofgarten,
> And drank coffee, and talked for an hour.
> Bin gar keine Russin, stamm 'aus Litauen, echt deutsch.
> And when we were children, staying at the archduke's,
> My cousin's, he took me out on a sled,
> And I was frightened. He said, Marie,
> Marie, hold on tight. And down we went.
> In the mountains, there you feel free.
> I read, much of the night, and go south in the winter.

153

Entry in Peruvian Journal

August 25th in the early morning we drive from the Hotel Allonte to the Cuzco Station to board the train to Juliaco and from there to Puno by car, then to Lake Titicaca. The early morning crowd of Quecheuan Indians, mestizos, tourists is neither as noisy nor as exotic as I expected, the train both better and worse. We climb onto the "buffet" car, expecting a first class something or other club and dining car, visions of wood panels and silverware, a rose bud beside the white table cloth, the old CPR into the mountains toward Banff, toward holidays in the mountains, only to find a battered green coach and ripped green leather seats in facing couples, ours a group of four at the rear of the coach. A news boy cries out something about death at Macchu Picchu but the paper we buy, *Le Chronica*, is yesterday's and we read of the official account of the New York Times' attempt to manoeuvre Peruvian credit to force some issue or another. The train moves through the brown, beige, red clay country of Cuzco, past the agricultural collectives, mediaeval huddlings of huts around old estate homes occupied by peasant farmers, by adobe villages, mud-dabbed and thatched hovels surrounded by a mud-brick wall, desert yielding to limestone crags. We are climbing, entering the Altiplano. The mountains recede, heights become meaningless, a vast bleak plain, the peaks rising above it on the horizon, stretches out. Los Reya at 14,000 feet, it is snowing, ponies and mules stand by the station facing away from the wind, heads down, men standing, their heads in wool ear-flap caps, oddly Mongolian, their feet bare, on the vast plateau moving toward Puno. Prophecies and miracles.

In the bitterly cold morning of snowflurries and wind-whipped waves the boat chugs out across the lake toward an Uru reed island, the reed huts like pointed caps, one other building visible, sheet metal or tin-sided, its sign soon discernable: ESCUELA FLOTANTE ADVENTISTA. Inside, growing clearer in the dark, a huge painted canvas, a Christ reaching out to bless the island, the children and the school:
EDUCAR ES REDIMIR.   That morning we leave Titicaca, 13,500 feet, climbing, to cross the Andes by car.

Late summer in Banff, the festival presents *Kiss Me, Kate.*

II THE POLITICS OF ART[2]

"Within certain limits, bad thoughts and bad morals can be good literature. If so great a man as Tolstoy could not demonstrate the contrary, I doubt whether anyone else can either." George Orwell said that in June, 1941. He was talking about what he called "the frontiers of art and propaganda," and I suggest it might be worthwhile to begin our discussions here today with the same subject in mind. That is because this seminar proposes to examine the possibility of a coherent cultural policy and so it must say something about the same limits Orwell sought to make clear. Those limits are implied in the very terms we use, whether politics and art or cultural policy. I share with Orwell the view that it might not be wrong, considering the place we live in, to demand litera-ture should first and foremost be propaganda. It will still be wrong to make what are ostensibly literary judgments for political ends. That is a distinction to get clear first of all and these remarks are directed to that end.

Every work of art is about its own limitations.
CITY-TV, 9:45 pm., Feb. 25, 1977

Bring it home. This place. This time. Questions about the politics of art are usually raised and have been raised under a variety of guises, as a question of style, a question of influence, a question of audience, a question of funding, or whatever. The terms I have heard most often in recent Canadian writing are those like international as opposed to na-tional, elitist as opposed to democratic, cosmopolitan as opposed to native, colonial as opposed to independent, *them* as opposed to *us*. The point is, whether it sounds abstract or not to put it this way, the distinctions seem real enough to anyone arguing questions of cultural policy in this country. They are distinctions that lie behind countless and continuing disputes in the formulation of Canada Council policy about the funding of the arts in Canada. You'll hear them in the paranoia of any regional conference of writing, especially in Western Canada. They perplex policy makers in schools or centres of the arts, like the one at York or the Centre at Banff. They are the stock in trade of cultural nationalists, the vocabulary of their magazines, the lingo of their busi-ness.

I'm not going to talk about the immediate history of positions that have been taken on questions of this sort, and I'm not going to present it as a conflict of personalities, though that is by far the most colourful and dramatic version it can take. Instead, I'll begin with a schematic view of the politics of art, more particularly writing, partly because it is, for me, a convenient way of getting past certain kinds of mystification that usually attend discussions of this sort, but also because I believe the urgent and real issues can be put schematically, and perhaps only in that way. The schematic view is this:

At one extreme, we find writing we call radical, at the other formalist. Obviously, there is room for all sorts of shading in between. For "radi-cal," you can read: marxist, leftist, engaged, or whatever; for "formalist" you can read: aesthetic, metaphysical, fantastic—or whatever. I've re-cently heard the distinction put as between an aesthetic of space and an aesthetic of time. Radical approaches insist on grounding writing in history, in time, within specific historical, political, economic and social *causes:* material reality. In Canada, this calls for a recognition of Ameri-canization as a political, economic, and cultural fact, and decolonization

155

as a programme. Formalist approaches find their cause, or the cause of writing, in literary forms. Northrop Frye provides the influential and instructive theory: poems imitate poems, forms derive from forms. The Argentinian Borges, whose essay "The Argentinian Writer and Tradition" might well be the sub-text for this position, points to the real meaning of formalism: literary forms are forms of fantasy, and fantasy tells us that the world is only our dream in which we ourselves are dreamt or dreaming. Radical aesthetics tends to regard "culture" as a superstructure. Its real cause is material and specific. Formal aesthetics tends to regard society, or material reality, as a formal element of literature: no more than any other necessity in a story, and no realer than a spell cast on the liberating creative power the work celebrates.

One further distinction I think will concern us most in these discussions: it has to do with purposes, and so in the end with programmes and policies. On the face of it, radical approaches call for a rapid movement from literary design toward practical and political solutions to the problem initiating a work. A formalist writer does not look for solutions at all, so much as disengagement or disinterestedness, at least so far as material causes are concerned. His interest is design itself. But no sooner is this question of practical ends raised than contradictions emerge.

Cultural nationalism offers the most important example. It arises from an historical and real condition. Presumably it calls for certain kinds of commitment on the part of the writer. But in fact, both in theory and practice, it now appears the drive of literary nationalism is toward a deeper and deeper exploration of the forms of its expression rather than to the nature of any proposed action; in other words, in precisely a direction opposite to what one might at first expect. I'm not saying there is a homogenous cultural nationalist position, nor a formulated propaganda programme, against which there has been a re-action. I am saying one can look at certain instructive examples of how writers have thought of their problem. I choose three: one in theatre, one in poetry, one in the Quebecois novel.

On Canadian theatre, Martin Kinch argues the mere presence of Canadian plays is no longer enough, the short term hit cannot substitute for the more serious concern, the urgent question is not substance but the creation of a strong dramatic experience, "the imaginative exploration of our life and our reality." In poetry, Dennis Lee turns the nationalist argument into a question of literary language, not to find a subject but a voice. Eloquently in "Cadence, Country, Silence," he tells of his struggle to find a language he would not strangle on, his own language, authentic in its sense of loss and locality. His theory of decolonization turns out to be as much a literary as a political solution. Form itself is here a political matter, a point to which I will return in a moment. Most strikingly, in Roch Carrier's Quebec trilogy, formal considerations outweigh questions about the material consequences of repression. Carrier's radical response to the colonization of Quebec is the creation of dream vision, grotesque and distorted imagery, the language of surrealism.[3] His position is not unlike the one Marcel Rioux describes in *Quebec in Question*. Citing the argument of d'allemagne, Rioux says, "Cultural colonialism is simply the result of economic and political colonialism." But the conclusions are not quite what we might expect:

> For some years now, especially since Jacques Breque published his ideas on the subject, many Quebecers have come to realize that socio-economic imperialism alters not only the language of the oppressed, but their whole culture and personality as well. As d'allemagne put it, "An oppressed people has no chance to be involved in the great realities, the great problems and the great decisions of life. Such a people can hardly help but express themselves badly; after all, what have they to express . . . except their solitude and rebellion?"

As in Lee's poetry, a formal response to social reality is here presented as a political response. Cultural life is defined in terms of its political dimensions.[4] It seems obvious and perhaps not even surprising; but still the other side of the argument, the formalist one, needs to be looked at.

The question is of more than theoretical interest. After all, the most influential kind of literary criticism in Canada, the thematic criticism of writers like Margaret Atwood and Doug Jones, derives from the work of Northrop Frye, himself an extraordinarily powerful cultural and political force and the foremost theoretician of the aesthetics of formalism. Frye, of course, developed at length and in detail an elaborate theory of an autonomous imagination and a disinterested and detached literary and critical theory, a formalist, humanist, and liberal theory of culture, education, and communications. To watch the evolution, perhaps one could say, the contortions, of his argument as he attempts to accommodate it to the concerns of writing in Canada, is a fascinating exercise and one that serves to bring the questions I have been talking of here into clearest focus. For my purposes here, I distinguish three different positions on Canadian writing in his work:

1) In the forties, Frye attempted a formalist analysis of a national literature. He sought to develop the view that there are distinctive Canadian forms, that there is a myth of the north in Canadian writing, and that there is something to be called "the Canadian imagination."

2) In the sixties, he chose to view Canada in the context of modernism with two surprising consequences: 1) Canada disappeared. Very few have noted that in *The Modern Century*, written on the occasion of the Canadian centenary, Frye not only showed an extraordinary indifference to the fate of Canada but explicitly argued that we are simply part of the American defense system, the real N/A boundary is not the 49th parallel but the northern defense system between

the bourgeois state (his term) and the marxist (his term) and in any event talk about the Canadian imagination, of the kind he indulged in earlier is, like theories of national culture, a piece of romantic folklore; and 2) the actual country is of less interest to him than some sort of ideal Canada, a place never to be realized, though perhaps worth striving after.

3) In the seventies, the context was no longer national nor modern but political and so Frye now tells us that the by-now-famous "Canadian imagination" is first of all purely fictional and second, always regional. Echoing arguments of liberal political theorists, he makes a distinction between culture and state. "Identity" he argues "is local and regional, rooted in imagination and works of culture; unity is national in reference, international in perspective, and rooted in political feeling."

There is no such place called Estevan, Venezuela.
Ottawa TV, 10:45 pm., Feb. 21, 1977

Nationalist, internationalist, regionalist. So distinguished a critic as Professor Frye might be permitted inconsistency but on what basis can a consistent argument for cultural policy then be developed by lesser mortals like ourselves? The problem or puzzle in Frye's work, and in radical critiques, is not, I think, confusion. Anything but. It has to do with the distinction between the *nature* of forms and their *source,* or more accurately, their *location.* Examine their nature and you move into the world of fantasy or the realm of the ideal. Look at their location and you see them in an historical context, in a given place and time. The first is a formalist approach; the second the radical. In either case, the unremitting tension between the two possibilities remains.

Is that an impasse? I don't think so. I think there are certain conclusions that any discussion of the politics of art ought to be mindful of:

1) Even the most radical argument about the arts must finally recognize something in art that goes beyond politics. I know how grudging the politicized writer is about this, but nonetheless, I cite Orwell once again: "Every piece of writing has its propaganda aspect, and yet in any book, or play, or poem, or what not that is to endure there has to be a residuum of something that simply is not affected by its moral or meaning—a residuum of something we call art."

2) By the same token, what I'll call the Mordecai Richler theory of writing is as wrong as the propagandist's. The Richler theory states simply what matters is whether a work is good, not whether it is Canadian. "Good" and "Canadian" in this view become contradictions in terms. But even the most rigorously formal argument must finally admit the extent to which writing is local, particular, regional, and therefore, in

Canadian terms, native in its concerns and interests.

3) It is time to dispense with the mythology that there is such a thing as "the Canadian imagination" and to recognize the degree to which writing in this country is regional. I suspect, though I can't argue it now, that the term "Canadian imagination" conceals a particularly vicious kind of centralism.

4) Arguments about the need for good writing tend to be elitist in intent. Arguments for regional writing tend to be populist.

5) and finally, neither the illiteracy of the politician nor the naivity of the writer should be allowed to carry the day. Theories of intellectuals are best ignored altogether.

There are dangers as well as confusions in these apparent conclusions, but much of this essay has been directed to style as well as ideology, and particularly to the question as to whether a radical politics and literature could ever afford to ignore style. In my terms, both the radical and formalist aesthetics converge at their deepest point of creative activity. Anything less, on either side is both brutal and exploitative. One knows the guise under which exploitation occurs: decorum, manners, civility, timidity, polish, gentility. But there is a better way of saying it. At what point do structures, ideologies, institutions themselves seem or feel threatened? For Agee, even and especially, the clown in his baggy pants, twirling cane, and irresponsibility, anarchist of the imagination, seemed always to be the one pursued through city streets endlessly by hordes of stick-swinging policemen, the law and order of a social society that felt threatened by *him*. And of course, finally they exiled him.

> Beheaded corpse man jailed.
> Headline *Toronto Star* January (?) 1977

III WAYS OUT OF BANFF

Entry in Peruvian Journal

On August 27 we are driving across the High Andes in a taxi, a 1965 (?) Dodge, battered, worse for the wear, the road a gravel track that disappears every now and again. We're in snow, only growth lichen, animals flit by, chinchilla, grazing alpaca, once astonishingly a flock of flamingoes in a deep valley, nothing else but remote peaks. At Patti, two adobe huts, a circular servicio, we stop for lunch, Fanta, two cokes, a Inca Kola, Ann. drinking coca leaves in hot water, at 16,000 feet, and we begin to descend as we pass the occasional truck hauling supplies back to Puno and Juliaco, once only another car as we wind down the switchbacks toward Aeroquipa, the driver leaning out asks of us in Spanish: "ARE WE GOING THE RIGHT WAY?"

What other way? I ask myself. How to get out of Banff:

take a car
take a cab
take a bus
take a train
write a book
write a poem
write a play
and how can we ever go back?

NOTES

1. Tunnel Mountain—elevation 5,500
   Cascade Mountain—elevation 9,836
   Rundle Mountain—9,834
   Sulphur Mountain—8,000 (approximately)

2. The comments in this section were addressed to a preseminar on
   "Art and Audience: toward a cultural policy," at York University on March
   30, 1977.

3. The argument here depends heavily on Ann Mandel's approach to her reading of Carrier, Kroetsch, and others in comments appearing in a
   proposed book on Canadian writers.

4. A marxist analysis of literary forms is, of course, possible (witness Lukacs'
   work on the history of the novel as genre) and what I say here about
   formalist aesthetic, I believe, is not inconsistent with such an analysis. But
   the question of creativity is another matter. To locate the source of
   literary forms in creative energy is probably romantic rather than anything
   else, but to see that source as potentially revolutionary rather than
   decorative suggests at least the kinds of meaning that can be attached to
   much of nineteenth century romanticism from Shelly and Beethoven
   to Goya.

Date Due

FORM 109			